THE NATURALLY CLEAN HOME

the NATURALLY
CLEAN HOME

150
Super-Easy
Herbal Formulas for
GREEN CLEANING

KARYN SIEGEL-MAIER

Storey Publishing

The mission of Storey Publishing is to serve our customers by publishing practical information that encourages personal independence in harmony with the environment.

Edited by Deborah Balmuth and Lizzie Stewart
Art direction and book design by Alethea Morrison
Text production by Liseann Karandisecky

Cover photography by © Susie Cushner
Illustrations by © Kim Rosen

Indexed by Nancy D. Wood

Printed in the United States by Dickinson Press
10 9 8 7 6 5 4 3 2 1

Library of Congress Cataloging-in-Publication Data
Siegel-Maier, Karyn, 1960–
  The naturally clean home / Karyn Siegel-Maier. — 2nd ed.
    p. cm.
  Includes index.
  ISBN 978-1-60342-085-3 (paper : alk. paper)
  1. House cleaning. 2. Household supplies. I. Title.
TX324.S24 2009
648'.5—dc22
                              2008035260

CONTENTS

This book is dedicated to you, the reader, whose commitment to better living is my inspiration and reward for living.

Acknowledgments

Warm thanks to my family, friends, and online community members for all the inspiration, feedback, and support over the years. Your encouragement is the driving force that motivates me every day.

I'd also like to express my appreciation for the honor of being a member of Storey's family of authors. In particular, special thanks to Deborah Balmuth and Lizzie Stewart for helping to give new life to these pages to reach a new generation of readers.

WHY CLEAN WITH HERBS?

NEARLY EVERYONE HAS HEARD ABOUT THE VIRTUES of common items such as baking soda and vinegar for cleaning jobs like scouring and absorbing grease. The addition of herbal materials, especially essential oils, to the formula serves to enhance its cleaning value with the added benefit of leaving behind a soothing, natural scent. In effect, the principles of sanitary hygiene and aromatherapy become partners. It's not by advertising gimmick that many commercial products contain citrus oils, such as lemon or lime; they are natural degreasers and have antimicrobial properties. In fact, citrus oils are the workhorses of the kitchen and bathroom. Many other herbs possess antibacterial and antifungal qualities as well. The chart on pages 26–27 gives more information on the beneficial cleaning properties of specific herbs.

The Benefits of Natural Cleaning

You can believe me when I tell you that using a natural herbal product instead of a chemical-laden commercial one makes household tasks almost a pleasure to tackle. I know it's hard to get excited about cleaning a bathroom, but when you realize that the surfaces are germ and toxin free, and the soothing aroma of cedar or lavender lingers, you won't be able to suppress a smile of satisfaction. And the enthusiasm is contagious — even the kids will want to pitch in!

Save Time and Money

Making your own herbal cleaning products is not a time-consuming or expensive endeavor. In fact, quite the opposite is true. It only takes a minute or two to fill a spray bottle with vinegar and water and add a few drops of essential oil. Bingo — instant glass and appliance cleaner! Having done that, there's one less aisle to visit in the supermarket.

The majority of commercial cleaners are quite expensive. A typical spray or foam cleanser for the bathroom, for instance, can deprive you of $4.00 or more. An herbal alternative, on the other hand, will cost mere pennies to make. I buy pure essential oils for an average of

$3.00 per half fluid ounce. Since I am only using between 5 and 30 drops of the oil (depending on the particular formula), that half-ounce bottle goes a very long way indeed. Other all-natural ingredients, such as vinegar, baking soda, water, and castile soap are also inexpensive.

Unclutter Your Cleaning Closet

You will also marvel at the amount of uncluttered space that becomes available in the area where you normally store cleaning supplies. According to Debra Lynn Dadd, author of *Nontoxic & Natural*, the average kitchen is home to thirty or more commercial products, the laundry room six!

Many of the herbal formulas you will be making will be multipurpose, so the number of cleaning products you store will be greatly reduced — an immense help to those of us with only a little bit of space under the sink or in a closet.

Creative Packaging

Why shouldn't the containers used to store your herbal cleaners be as pleasant as their contents? In this area, you can really exercise the concept of recycling materials. Remember those commercial products you finished up on your way to nontoxic cleaning? Many of those containers can be washed and used a countless number of times for your herbal formulas.

Coffee tins with plastic lids are great for storing car and wood polishes. Those large plastic containers with sprinkle-type tops you get when you purchase dried herbs and spices in bulk are excellent for powdered cleansers. Glass containers work well too, of course, but you may want to stick with plastic if safety is a concern, especially if your little helpers may be using them.

Which Herbs to Use

The formulas in this book suggest combinations of dried herbs and essential oils. Herb substitutions are encouraged when necessitated. The chart on pages 26–27 can help you make your selection according to the desired cleaning action.

For the most part, essential oils are suitable for all-purpose cleaning, floor and furniture care, and laundry needs. Strong tinctures can be used in place of essential oils in some formulas, if necessary, but their cleaning power will be less effective if used in laundry recipes, or those intended to be antibacterial. For obvious reasons, dried herbal material won't do for these tasks, but are excellent for other jobs such as scouring tubs and sinks and for use in carpet fresheners.

Purchasing Essential Oils

Essential oils and dried herbs are readily available in health food stores and by mail order. See Resources for a listing of good mail-order suppliers that sell both. But before you make any purchase, you should know that there are differences between herbal oils. Make sure that you're buying a pure, undiluted essential oil and not one that has been diluted in a carrier oil. Aromatherapy oils are a dilution of one or more essential oils with a carrier oil, such as almond or jojoba, and are intended for massage work and making perfume, among other things.

There are even grade differences among pure essential oils, but this difference generally pertains to the quality of fragrance, and for the purpose of household cleaning it is insignificant. Price may vary considerably as well, depending on the plant, its availability, and the extraction process.

Your essential oils will come in either blue or brown glass bottles. If stored away from heat and direct light, some essential oils will retain their potency indefinitely. Citrus oils are an exception; they usually last for about one year. Oil bottles usually come with droppers already built into the cap. The built-in dropper is there for a reason: to help you measure out the oil easily and control the number of drops you use. Use only the amount of essential oil called for in a recipe. The oils are highly concentrated, and adding more won't make a superstrong formula; instead, it can increase the risk of skin irritation.

Keep in mind that essential oils can irritate the skin and must be diluted with a carrier oil or other liquid before use. Always practice caution when handling essential oils, and never allow children to handle the pure oils. Wearing protective gloves is highly recommended if your skin will be coming into contact with the chosen cleaner.

Can I Make My Own Essential Oils?

The best quality essential oils are often made by steam distillation. Unless you're a complete naturalist with plenty of time on your hands, making essential oils at home can be costly and tedious. However, many herbal supply companies offer home stills in a variety of sizes and with a price range of $50 to more than $100. Either way, it still takes a hefty amount of plant material to extract a small vial full of essential oil. Personally, I find this idea impractical for my lifestyle and prefer to buy my oils.

Choosing the Oils to Use

Which essential oils do you need? I use a variety of oils in cleaning formulas simply because I enjoy many different scents and because I keep a varied supply on hand for other projects. You may decide to use only a handful, and that's fine. Here are the most common essentials oils called for in the formulas in this book:

* Cedar
* Citronella
* Eucalyptus
* Lavender
* Lemon
* Lime
* Mint (including peppermint, spearmint, and wintergreen)
* Pine
* Rosemary
* Sweet orange
* Tea tree

Growing Your Own Herbs

If you are fortunate enough to be able to grow your own herbs, as I do, you will already have a supply of herbal material on hand to dry for making scouring powders, sachets, and carpet fresheners. The dried flowers and leaves of many herbs — such as rosemary, sage, lavender, mint, and lemon balm — are suitable for these products. Most herbs are quite hardy, easy to grow, and add beauty to any lawn or garden. Let's not forget the contributions they make to meals!

You will need to dry the herbs before using them in cleaning formulas. The concentration of essential oils is highest just before and during flowering. You'll want to leave at least one-third of each perennial in the garden to ensure its return the following season.

Harvesting Herbs

The leaves and stems can be harvested by cutting into stalks just before or during flowering, when their essential oils are at their peak. Flowers can be used too, and they will be at their best at either the bud stage or in full bloom. Rose, lavender, and rosemary blossoms are all harvested this way, and are especially good additions to powdered cleansers.

Roots, rhizomes, and bulbs should be taken from biennials and perennials when their oils and nutrients are not being used for the plant's growth. This occurs during late summer or fall when the plant begins to die back and store nutrients underground for the winter, or in early spring as the first leaves begin to emerge. Ginger is a popular herb that is harvested in this manner.

Drying Herbs

The old-fashioned and most pleasant way to dry herbs is the method of air-drying. At the end of each summer, I cut several stalks of different herbs to hang in my kitchen to dry. The aroma is incredible! Unless you have a perfectly controlled climate, attics, basements, and garages are usually either too arid or too moist to dry herbs in. Moisture can cause molding, and you'll have to start over.

The key to air-drying successfully is to hang the herbs upside down in small bunches (four or five medium-size stalks each) and to provide a place where they will get sufficient air circulation and be sheltered from direct sunlight and extreme temperatures. Secure the stalks fairly tightly with string or ribbon; they shrink somewhat during the drying process and tend to slip away from the bunch. You don't want to find your herbs on the floor! You also might want to write the name of the plant on a small tag and attach it to the stalks. Unless you're familiar with herbs and their different scents, you might get confused about the identity of the dried product.

Ideally, herbs should hang freely from cup hooks or pegs to dry. No room in your kitchen? There's always the ceiling — they won't be in anyone's way up there. Special racks can be constructed or purchased for this purpose. Some people spread herbs out on screens to dry — fine solution, as long as you have the room and you do not expose the herbs to extreme heat or moisture.

In two to three weeks, the herbs should feel very dry and the leaves can then be stripped away from the stalk and crumbled into clean glass jars. Avoid storing dried herbs in plastic bags because the volatile oils of the herb will interact with the chemicals in the plastic.

Another method of drying herbs is in a food dehydrator. This method is excellent, because the plants dry evenly, as long as you don't pack the trays with too much material. Such quick drying preserves the essential oils, and you'll have the added benefit of dried herbs within a matter of hours instead of weeks. I bought my five-tier dehydrator at a garage sale a few years back. It was the best $2.00 I've ever spent. By the way . . . why not hang a few sprigs of herbs to air-dry in the kitchen anyway, just to capture the spirit of your craft? Their aroma will last for months and they lend a homey feel when on display.

I don't recommend drying herbs in the oven. Even at a low temperature setting, the herbs dry too quickly, their oils evaporate due to constant heat radiation, and they easily scorch.

Other Methods of Preserving Herbs

While drying is the most common and basic way to preserve herbs, there are several other methods you might wish to try due to space limitations or other concerns, such as a damp climate. The following are some of the more popular preservation techniques.

Infusions are like very strong teas. The herbal material, including flowers, is steeped in boiling water for at least 10 minutes, then strained and poured into clean containers. A general guide is one tablespoon of herb to each cup of water. Infusions can be used in a formula in place of water; rosemary, thyme, and oregano infusions are very helpful when used this way. When kept in the refrigerator, an infusion will last two to three weeks.

Decoctions are made to extract the essential oils from heavier materials, such as roots and bark. The herbal material is simmered for 10 to 30 minutes and the liquid then strained. Use about one ounce of herb to each cup water. Like 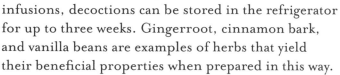 infusions, decoctions can be stored in the refrigerator for up to three weeks. Gingerroot, cinnamon bark, and vanilla beans are examples of herbs that yield their beneficial properties when prepared in this way.

Tinctures, also called extracts, are a 1:1 solution of alcohol and water. (Vinegar is sometimes used in place of alcohol.) With this method, the herbal material is packed into a jar and completely covered with a solution of 50 percent alcohol (or vinegar) and 50 percent water and left to stand on a sunny shelf for two to three weeks. It helps to gently shake or turn the jar once a day to redistribute its contents. Tinctures may be used in cleaning formulas, but add only ½ ounce at a time. Because of the alcohol content, too much tincture in a formula can be irritating to both the lungs and skin.

Vinegars are made in the same manner as tinctures, but the vinegar is used full strength.

Common Cleaning Toxins

There is no shortage of documentation to prove that many common household products are dangerous to the environment and your health. But there are several readily available all-natural alternatives that will make letting go of your familiar standby products painless. Some of these items you probably already have on hand. Other items can be found in most natural foods stores, hardware stores, and supermarkets.

Soap vs. Detergent

Before the dawn of large-scale manufacturing, liquid soaps were made from saponins: foaming, sudsy substances found in the roots of soapwort, soapberry, and yucca. The typical liquid dishwashing soap bought from the grocery store is made from a petroleum distillate, a toxic pollutant and nonrenewable resource. This product is actually a detergent, not soap. The safe and natural alternative is a vegetable-based soap called castile, a pure soap made from coconut or olive oil. It is readily biodegradable and made from renewable sources.

Castile soap can be found in liquid or solid form in health food stores and, thankfully, some supermarkets. One of the best known brands (and my personal favorite) is Dr. Bronner's, which comes in concentrated form and often pretreated with herbal oils. The company also allots at least 10 percent of its profits to rain-forest preservation and homeless shelter support. Does the manufacturer of your commercial liquid detergent do the same?

The Dangers of Bleach

Bleach, or sodium hypochlorite, is a combination of chlorine and sodium hydroxide (caustic soda) and is perhaps one of the most difficult of commercial cleaning products to relinquish. Technically speaking, household bleach is not considered corrosive or toxic, even if ingested. It is however, classified as a skin and eye irritant. It can burn human tissue, internally or externally, especially in small children. In fact, the accidental swallowing of bleach is the most frequently received call at Poison Control Centers involving children under the age of six. But young, tender hands and lips can also suffer serious burns.

If household bleach can do such damage, and is so predominantly a factor in the accidental poisoning of young children, why keep it around the house? There are many natural and nontoxic solutions for removing stains and keeping whites white. If you feel you must have access to a bottle of bleach, at least use one that is free of chlorine to reduce the risks. One of the best that I have used is made by Seventh

Generation. Although the company doesn't supply its products on a retail level, they can often be found in health food stores and in some supermarkets. Treat this bleach as you would any other: store it in a locked cabinet or out of reach of pets and children.

A WORD ABOUT SAFETY

Although the ingredients you will be using to make cleaning formulas are of organic origin, that doesn't mean they are without consequences if ingested.

Essential oils are highly concentrated forms of the volatile oils found in plants and should never be used internally. Just a few drops are equivalent to approximately 30 or 40 cups of herbal tea. Take special care with food-related oils; citrus oil, for example, could offer a temptation to a young child who may mistake a finished product as something delicious to eat or drink. Essential oils, and other materials you find recommended in this book, can be irritating to the skin.

Please exercise the same caution with our herbal cleaning formulas as you would any commercial cleaner, and keep them away from pets and children.

Getting Started

Now that you've decided to switch to all-natural cleaning products, you might be wondering what you need to get started. The following must-have items will create a large variety of cleaners for all sorts of different surfaces and jobs.

Supplies at a Glance

The basic supplies required for making your own cleaners are generally inexpensive and easy to find. To make the widest array of products for the home, the following are the items to have on hand.

Baking soda. Otherwise known as bicarbonate of soda, you can find this ingredient very inexpensively at any supermarket or grocery store, usually in the baking supplies aisle.

Beeswax. This solid substance, usually in chunk or brick form, is available at art and craft stores, candle supply shops, and sometimes from local beekeepers.

Borax. A combination of water, oxygen, sodium, and boron, borax is a powder sold in the laundry aisle of grocery stores. A popular brand is 20 Mule Team by the Dial Corporation.

Carnauba wax. The hardest natural wax known, made from a Brazilian palm tree, this item is sold by furniture stores and mail-order companies.

Castile soap. An important ingredient, liquid castile soap is sold at health food stores, some supermarkets, and via mail order.

Citrus seed extract. Usually made from grapefruit seed, this natural preservative is a powerful antimicrobial agent. It is often sold as grapefruit seed extract, and sometimes as liquid Paramycocidin, and is available through mail order, as well as at some health food stores.

Cream of tartar. A popular culinary ingredient, this powdered mixture is sold in a box in the herb and spice or baking aisle of any supermarket.

Diatomaceous earth. This powder, made from the skeletons of fossilized algae, is available at garden supply and hardware stores, as well as through mail-order companies. Note, however, that this type of diatomaceous earth is not the same substance that you can buy from pool supply centers.

Essential oils. These concentrated volatile oils of plants can be found at health food stores, specialty shops, and via mail order.

Glycerin. Glycerin is a useful liquid for cleaners, medicines, and even some craft projects. You'll find it at art and craft stores, some pharmacies, and natural food stores.

Lanolin. Lanolin, an oily substance derived from sheep's wool, can be purchased from mail-order companies.

Murphy's Oil Soap. A very popular liquid soap for wood, Murphy's is sold at just about any supermarket. Check the cleaning products aisle.

Soap Flakes. Order from MSO Distributing or Soaps Gone Buy (see Resources) or buy pure soap at the health food store and grate it yourself.

Washing soda. Washing soda's generic name is sodium carbonate, and it's also known as soda ash. Some supermarkets stock Arm & Hammer's Super Washing Soda in the laundry products aisle. If yours doesn't, you can purchase it online (see Resources).

White vinegar. Used in many cuisines, white vinegar is found in the oil aisle of any supermarket.

Suggested Equipment

Many of these implements may already be on hand. Wash and rinse the containers from your old products and they're ready to service you again in your non-toxic cleaning chores. Be sure to label your product with a list of ingredients; any type of label from an office supply, stationery, or grocery store will do. While you're at it, be creative and give your formula a catchy name! Since labels can get wet, they are best covered with clear shipping tape or laminating sheets cut to size. Plan to keep the following around:

Plastic squirt bottles. You will need various sizes, depending on the purpose.

Plastic spray bottles. Get both small and large sizes.

Plastic containers with shaker tops. Spice containers are great.

Misters (plastic pump spray bottles).

Coffee cans with lids. These are great for storing waxes and pastes.

Glass jars. Preferably get wide-mouthed jars with screw-top lids.

Cotton cloths. Use cloths instead of paper towels.

Rags. T-shirts, scrap cotton cloth, and old towels are examples of good rags for cleaning.

Cellulose sponge cloth. Made of natural cellulose, these are absorbent, nonscratching, washable, and durable.

Gallon-size buckets. For large jobs.

Mops. Use a cotton-head mop for floors and a sponge-head mop for carpets and walls.

MAKING A STARTER KIT

If you're just starting out and don't have any essential oils, then here's a list of "essential essentials" that will be easy on your budget and that you can always add to later:

* Citronella
* Citrus (lemon, lime, or sweet orange)
* Tea tree
* Wintergreen (take extra care when handling)

The herbs that are the most helpful to have on hand are:

* Basil
* Lavender
* Lemon balm
* Mint
* Oregano
* Rosemary
* Sage
* Thyme

Herbs and Their Beneficial Properties

Many herbs have antibiotic, antiviral, antiseptic, and antifungal properties. The following list is not complete by any means, but it represents the most common herbs that are grown in home gardens and that are easily available in dried or essential-oil form.

HERB	PROPERTIES
Bay	antibacterial
Bergamot	antibiotic
Camphor	antibacterial
Cardamom	antibacterial
Chamomile	antibiotic, antibacterial
Cinnamon	antiviral
Citronella	antibacterial
Clove	antibiotic, antiviral
Cypress	antibacterial
Eucalyptus	antibiotic, antifungal, antiviral, antibacterial
Ginger	antibacterial
Hyssop	antifungal, antibacterial
Juniper	antifungal, antibacterial
Lavender	antibiotic, antifungal, antiviral, antibacterial
Lemon	antibiotic, antifungal, antiviral, antibacterial
Lemongrass	antibacterial

Lemon verbena	antibacterial
Lime	antibiotic, antibacterial
Marjoram	antibacterial
Myrtle	antibiotic, antifungal
Nutmeg	antibiotic
Orange	antibacterial
Oregano	antibiotic, antiviral
Patchouli	antibiotic, antifungal
Pine	antibiotic, antibacterial
Rosemary	antibacterial
Sage	antifungal, antibacterial
Sandalwood	antifungal, antiviral, antibacterial
Savory	antifungal
Spearmint	antibacterial
Tea tree	antibiotic, antifungal, antiviral, antibacterial
Thyme	antibacterial, antifungal, antiviral,
Vervain	antibacterial
Wintergreen	antibacterial; take extra care when handling

THE KITCHEN

TO ME, THE KITCHEN IS THE HUB AND HEART of a home. This room is more than a storage receptacle for culinary sundries; it's where we gather with cherished family and friends for mealtime celebrations. Unfortunately, it's also the room where the garbage is usually kept, where a bare floor endures the patter of muddy feet, and where the odor of grease and last night's fish stubbornly linger. In other words, it's a haven for germs. Save for the loo, the kitchen is probably the most frequented room in the house and is most in need of daily cleaning.

It's a pity that most of us grew up to think a clean kitchen is only evidenced by the overwhelming and pungent smell of a pine solvent. And little did we realize that our nervous systems were being treated to an assault of toxins. But you can create your own cost-effective, healthy alternatives to all the kitchen cleaners you're accustomed to using.

Washing the Dishes

Dishwashing liquids and automatic dishwasher detergents have been designed to lure the consumer with their stimulating lemony scent. Their aromatic choice is more than an advertising gimmick; sure, citrus oils smell nice, but they are also natural degreasers. It's the rest of the ingredients in these harsh detergents that we are better off without.

Dishwashing Liquids

The herbal essential oils recommended in the following formulas will pack a punch on germs and greasy dirt without knocking you out in the process.

Fruity Dishwashing Blend

This blend will have you looking forward to washing dishes!

    liquid castile soap
15 drops lemon or lemongrass essential oil
6   drops lavender essential oil
5   drops bergamot essential oil

Fill a clean 22-ounce plastic squirt bottle with castile soap (diluted according to directions if using concentrate). Add the essential oils. Shake the bottle before each use. Add 1 to 2 tablespoons of the liquid to dishwater and wash as usual.

Citrus Dishwashing Blend

Here's another sweet–smelling formula.

- liquid castile soap
- 20 drops lime essential oil
- 10 drops sweet orange essential oil
- 5 drops citrus seed extract

Fill a clean 22-ounce plastic squirt bottle with castile soap (diluted according to directions if using concentrate). Add the essential oils and extract. Shake the bottle before each use. Add 1 to 2 tablespoons of the liquid to dishwater and wash as usual.

Herbal Dishwashing Blend

Enjoy the leafy–fresh fragrance as you wash!

- liquid castile soap
- 10 drops lavender essential oil
- 8 drops rosemary essential oil
- 4 drops eucalyptus essential oil

Fill a clean 22-ounce plastic squirt bottle with castile soap (diluted according to directions if using concentrate). Add the essential oils. Shake the bottle before each use. Add 1 to 2 tablespoons of the liquid to dishwater and wash as usual.

Dishwashing Blues Blend

Try this recipe for an uplifting washing experience.

> liquid castile soap
> 10 drops lemon essential oil
> 6 drops bergamot essential oil
> 4 drops lavender essential oil
> 2 drops orange essential oil

Fill a clean 22-ounce plastic squirt bottle with castile soap (diluted according to directions if using concentrate). Add the essential oils. Shake the bottle before each use. Add 1 to 2 tablespoons of the liquid to dishwater and wash as usual.

DON'T GIVE UP ON THE TOUGH JOBS

* *For very greasy dishes,* add ½ cup vinegar or lemon juice to the dishwater.
* *To loosen baked-on food from pots and pans,* immediately add some baking soda and wait 15 minutes before cleaning. If the pot or pan has cooled before you've had a chance to add baking soda, boil a solution of 1 cup water, 5 drops cedar or other essential oil, and 3 tablespoons baking soda directly in the pot or pan. Allow the mixture to stand until the food can be scraped off easily.

Automatic Dishwasher Detergents

When the first edition of this book was published, I wasn't very confident back then in offering automatic dishwasher formulas that could be made at home that would actually work, let alone be cost effective. Well, that's changed! Here are several easy-to-make formulas for your automatic dishwasher that will get the job done for just pennies per load.

Lavender Lift Automatic Dishwasher Powder

Enjoy the subtle fragrance of this formula while your dishes are being cleaned.

- **2 cups washing soda**
- **2 cups borax**
- **20 drops lavender essential oil**

Combine all ingredients, taking care to blend in the essential oil well. Store in a plastic container. Use 2 tablespoons per load of dishes.

Super Easy Automatic Dishwasher Powder

This formula is effortless to make, and since it stores well it can be doubled or made in bulk.

- **2 cups washing soda**
- **1 cup borax**
- **1 cup baking soda**

Combine all ingredients and store in a plastic container. To use, add about 2 tablespoons to the soap compartment of your dishwasher. If you find your glasses are getting a residue buildup, then reduce this amount to 1½ tablespoons.

Citrus Sparkle Automatic Dishwasher Powder

Citric acid is available in powdered form from many health food stores, stores that cater to home brewers of beer and wine, soap-making supply outlets and, of course, from various online sources. It is sometimes labeled as "sour salt."

- **2 cups washing soda**
- **2 cups borax**
- **6 tablespoons citrus acid powder**
- **25 drops grapefruit essential oil**

Combine all ingredients in a plastic container or tub and mix completely. Use 2 tablespoons per load of dishes.

Rescue Rinse for Hard Water

If you frequently find spots on your glasses or flatware, then you might want to try this simple remedy:

Add 1 cup white distilled vinegar to the rinse compartment of your dishwasher.

Tea Time for Two

Tea contains tannic acid, which will help to breakdown and remove soap residue from your dishes during the rinse cycle.

2   cups green or white tea

Brew two fresh cups of green or white tea. Add one cup to the rinse compartment of your dishwasher and relax while sipping the remaining cup.

The Kitchen Sink

The baking soda–essential oil mixtures in the following formulas can be made in larger batches and stored in a plastic container, glass jar, or coffee can (store the vinegar separately). I find the large plastic spice and herb jars with shaker tops are perfect for powdered cleaners. Just soak off the label and wash and dry the inside of the container.

Basic Sink Cleanser

This formula is safe for porcelain or stainless steel sinks. Not only will it clean the sink basin and faucets, but it will also keep drains and garbage disposals fresh-smelling and free of clogs. Note: *A vinegar rinse can be used before the final hot water rinse to prevent residue from the baking soda.*

- ¼ cup baking soda
- ½ cup vinegar
- 3 drops lavender, rosemary, lemon, lime, or orange essential oil

Combine all ingredients. Rinse sink well with hot water. Pour the cleanser in the sink and wipe with a sponge or cloth. Rinse again with hot water.

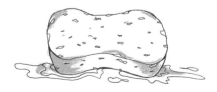

Herbal Scrubber

You can make up this formula in larger batches and store it in an airtight container. Use only whole dried (not powdered) plant material for this recipe.

- ½ cup baking soda
- ½ cup dried sage leaves, coarsely ground
- ¼ cup rosemary leaves, ground

Combine all ingredients in an airtight container and shake well to blend. Sprinkle a small amount of the powder into the sink and scrub with a damp sponge. Rinse well.

Country Spice Scrubber

Simple and sweet!

- 1 cup baking soda
- 3 teaspoons ground cinnamon
- 3 drops cedar or sweet orange essential oil

Combine all ingredients in an airtight container and shake well to blend. Sprinkle a small amount of the powder into the sink and scrub with a damp sponge. Rinse well.

Sink Scrubber for Stains

For stubborn stains, allow this formula to rest on the stain for several minutes. Then scrub and rinse with vinegar and hot water.

- ¼ cup borax
- ¼ cup baking soda
- 8 drops rosemary, eucalyptus, or tea tree essential oil
- ¾ cup vinegar for rinsing

Combine the borax, baking soda, and essential oil in an airtight container and shake well to blend. Sprinkle a small amount of the powder into the sink and scrub with a damp sponge. Rinse sink with vinegar, then with hot water.

Porcelain Sink Saver

If you have an old-fashioned porcelain sink in your kitchen then you know that even though they look lovely, they do take on scuff marks and stains rather easily. Try this herbal remedy for really stubborn spots.

- 1 part sage, rosemary, lemon balm, thyme, or mint, fresh or dried
- 1 part water

Brew a strong infusion by steeping the herb in hot water for 2 to 3 hours. Strain, reserving the liquid. Close the sink drain, pour in the liquid, and allow it to work for several hours or overnight. *Note:* If the stain persists, place 4 to 6 drops of your favorite essential oil directly on the stain for a few minutes and then scrub the spot with baking soda sprinkled on a damp sponge.

Rust Remover

Wipe away these unattractive stains with a fresh-scented cleaner.
Note: *If the stain is on the side of your sink, use more baking soda to make a thick paste that will cling to the spot.*

- ¼ cup baking soda
- 5 drops essential oil of choice
- juice of half a lemon

Sprinkle baking soda directly on the rust stain. Add essential oil and sprinkle with lemon juice. Allow the mixture to sit on the stain undisturbed for several hours or overnight. Wipe away baking soda and rinse thoroughly.

SIMPLE SINK CLEANSER
Bon Ami brand cleanser is made of grated detergent and feldspar and is nontoxic and nonabrasive. Sprinkle it freely in the sink basin and add 5 or 6 drops essential oil of choice, if desired. Scrub and rinse well.

Oven Cleaners

Commercial oven cleaners are one of the most toxic and unpleasant products you could use. If the fumes from the application aren't bad enough, the foul smell of chemical burn-off the stuff continues to produce is enough to make one afraid of turning on the oven! The following formulas work very well. No oven cleaner is a miracle worker, however. Sometimes it may require a bit of elbow grease if there's a great deal of buildup on your oven walls and floor.

When vinegar is added to baking soda, a fizzing reaction occurs. While this might startle you at first, it is perfectly normal.

SOAK THOSE STOVE ACCESSORIES!

The chrome rings that surround burners on an electric stove, the grills that rest on gas stove burners, and oven knobs all collect grease and food splatters over time. While cleaning your oven, these items can soak in a solution of 1 cup of baking soda, ½ cup vinegar, and 4 to 6 drops essential oil of your choice. Use a fine steel wool pad or old toothbrush to remove grime from small spaces.

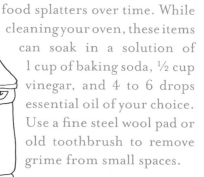

Serious Oven-Cleaning Formula

I once made a family-size turkey potpie in one of my best crocks and watched helplessly as it began bubbling over within minutes of putting it in the oven. What a mess! This formula is great for such disasters, or for ovens that have been neglected for a while. Note: *If you have a lot of baked-on grease or food splatters, you may want to use fine steel wool to scrub those areas. Use a bit more salt if necessary.*

½   cup salt
¼   cup washing soda or borax
1   box (16 ounces) baking soda
scant ¼ cup water
¾   cup white vinegar
10 drops thyme essential oil
10 drops lemon or lemongrass essential oil

1. Combine salt, washing soda, and baking soda in a plastic container or glass bowl. Add just enough water to make a paste.
2. Remove oven racks and preheat the oven to 250°F for 15 minutes, then turn off the oven and leave the door open.
3. Carefully spread the paste on oven walls with a sponge or cloth and allow to set for 20 to 30 minutes.
4. Combine the vinegar and essential oils in a spray bottle and shake well. Spray the oven walls and wipe clean. Rinse well.

Overnight Oven Cleaner

Bring out these proven grease–cutting oils for those heavy–duty oven–cleaning jobs.

1   cup water, divided
10 drops sweet orange, lemon, or rosemary essential oil
½   cup salt, divided
1¼ cups baking soda, divided
2   teaspoons liquid castile soap
¼   cup vinegar

1. Block the vents in the oven floor with aluminum foil or waxed paper. Preheat oven to 300°F for 15 minutes, then turn off the oven and leave the door open.

2. Combine ¼ cup of the water with essential oil in a plastic spray bottle and shake well. Spray oven floor and walls with this precleaning mixture.

3. Combine ¼ cup of the salt and ½ cup of the baking soda. Sprinkle the mixture on oven floor, paying particular attention to spill areas.

4. Mix ¼ cup of the water with the remaining baking soda (¾ cup) and salt (¼ cup), and the castile soap. Spread this mixture on the oven walls. Remove the foil or waxed paper from the vents and allow the paste to sit overnight.

5. In the morning, combine the remaining ½ cup water with the vinegar in a plastic spray bottle. Spray the oven walls and floor generously with this mixture. Wipe well, using fine steel wool to work off any stubborn spots. Rinse several times to remove any residue.

Sunday Oven-Cleaning Formula

This formula is for regular oven maintenance.

- **2 tablespoons baking soda**
- **2 tablespoons liquid castile soap**
- **10 drops sweet orange, lemon, or lime essential oil**
- **½ cup hot water**

1. Preheat oven to 250°F for 15 minutes, then turn off and leave door open.
2. Combine the baking soda, castile soap, and essential oil in a clean plastic spray bottle. Add the water and shake well.
3. Spray on oven walls and wait 20 minutes. Wipe clean and rinse well.

KEEP THOSE CABINETS SPARKLING

If you have Formica cabinets in your kitchen, you can clean them with an all-purpose cleaner such as any of the formulas in this section. The kitchen cabinets in our home are made of oak; for these I use a mixture of 2 cups water, ¼ cup Murphy's Oil Soap, and 15 to 20 drops of cedar or patchouli essential oil. The scent is heavenly — clean and woodlike.

Cleaning Kitchen Surfaces

Kitchen appliances, such as refrigerators, microwave ovens, and dishwashers, can get grimy from cooking grease and odors. Let's not forget those little fingerprints that magically appear on cabinet doors! The following formulas will clean without scratching surfaces, and can be made in larger batches and stored in plastic spray bottles.

Lemon Blast Cleaner

This solution is great for refrigerators and stove tops.

1	teaspoon liquid castile soap
⅛	cup white vinegar
¼	cup lemon juice
2	cups water
6	drops citrus seed extract
4	drops lemon, lime, orange, or eucalyptus essential oil
1	teaspoon borax

Combine all ingredients in a plastic spray bottle. Shake well before each use. Spray generously on appliance surface and wipe with a damp cloth or sponge. Wipe dry with a cloth or towel.

Herbal Degreaser

This formula will remove greasy film from appliance surfaces.

2   cups water
¼   cup oil-based soap (Murphy's is good)
10 drops rosemary, lavender, or citrus essential oil

Combine all ingredients in a plastic spray bottle. Shake well before each use. Spray generously on appliance surface and wipe with a damp cloth or sponge. Wipe dry with a cloth or towel.

Microwave Cleaner

The interior of a microwave oven can trap grease and cooking odors that can spoil the flavor of foods during cooking. Try this remedy whenever you think your microwave could use a little sprucing up. If your microwave has a glass turntable, remove it and wash by hand.

¼   cup baking soda
1   teaspoon vinegar
5–6 drops thyme, lemongrass, or lemon essential oil

Combine all ingredients to make a paste. Apply to the walls and floor of the microwave with a soft cloth or sponge. Rinse well and leave the microwave door open to air-dry for about 25 minutes.

Refrigerator & Freezer Rescue

We all have the best of intentions when we pack away those little containers of leftover foods and store them in the refrigerator. But often these receptacles are forgotten and the telltale aroma of something well past its prime soon makes its presence known, just a bit too late. Odors due to expired foods, or even up-to-date pungent smelling foods (like some cheeses) can create an offensive odor noticeable whenever the refrigerator door is opened. Strong odors can also affect fresh foods in both the refrigerator and the freezer.

If an unfriendly fragrance has permeated your freezer, remove all the contents and put them on ice in a cooler temporarily. If you have a separate temperature control for the freezer, turn it down for a few minutes. (If there isn't a separate control, leave the freezer door open for 5 minutes.) Wipe the interior of the freezer with a soft cloth dampened with a solution of ½ cup water, 3 tablespoons baking soda, and 6 drops eucalyptus or peppermint essential oil. Rinse well to remove any baking soda residue, and dry the walls, shelves, and floor of the freezer thoroughly with a tea towel before replacing food. Don't forget to turn the temperature control setting back up!

For refrigerator odors, you can use the solution recommended above to wipe down the walls, shelves, and doors, but increase the amount of essential oil to 10 drops.

Maintaining Freshness

If you just want to maintain freshness in the refrigerator, try one of these scented solutions:

Vanilla. Pour 2 ounces of vanilla extract (imitation is okay) into a small, shallow bowl or saucer and place it on a lower shelf for a few days.

Coffee. If you like the smell of coffee, place a bowl of ½ cup ground coffee on a shelf. This will last for several weeks. You can add 5 to 7 drops of essential oil or even ground herbs, such as vanilla bean, sarsaparilla, mace, or ginger.

If you have a persistent odor in the refrigerator, try one of these tips:

Citrus. Line the bottom shelf with newspaper that has been sprinkled with 10 to 15 drops of essential oil, such as lemon, lime, grapefruit, or sweet orange. Remove after 2 or 3 days.

Herb. If you have an herb garden currently in bloom, cut a few stems of fragrant plants such as sage, rosemary, lemon balm, or mint. Tie with string and hang from one of the racks. The fresh herbs should last for 2 to 3 weeks.

Unscented. A slice of bread left on a plate will absorb many odors. You can sprinkle the bread slice with 2 to 4 drops of essential oil of your choice for extra deodorizing power.

Controlling Kitchen Pests

Even the cleanest kitchens are susceptible to unwanted visitors. Give bugs the boot with these quick remedies.

Ants. Wipe out your kitchen cabinets with a damp sponge and 6 to 8 drops of peppermint or citronella essential oil. Then place 3 to 5 drops of those essential oils on windowsills, doorway cracks, and in the corners of the cabinet under your kitchen sink.

Centipedes, earwigs, and silverfish. Place several drops of peppermint, wintergreen, eucalyptus, or citronella essential oil in areas that collect moisture, such as damp basements, garages, and cabinets that house plumbing fixtures.

Cockroaches. Sprinkle a mixture of borax and sugar in the dark areas where roaches like to hide, but this method might not be feasible if you have young children or pets. It may be best to consult an exterminator.

Mice. Place several sprigs of fresh peppermint between pantry items in your cabinets, or make a solution of 2 cups water and 3 teaspoons of peppermint essential oil and spray it wherever you find mouse droppings.

Mites and weevils. Place a few whole nutmegs in flour bins or bags.

Other insects. Place loose bay leaves in your kitchen cabinets.

The Kitchen Floor

My sympathy goes to you if you chose or inherited light-colored flooring in your kitchen. With three boys, two cats, and a dog in our house, the kitchen traffic is nonstop and our old white flooring didn't keep any secrets about where they'd been. Thankfully, we now have multicolored patterned flooring in the kitchen that hardly shows a thing. Still, regardless of what kind of flooring there is in your kitchen it needs frequent washing, especially if there are human "floor dwellers" in your home. You can rest assured knowing that in addition to keeping your floor looking its best, these formulas are safe for young children who frequently crawl on them.

GET RID OF SCUFF MARKS
To remove scuff marks, apply 2 to 4 drops essential oil neat (undiluted) and wipe clean with a cloth. Rinse with a dash of vinegar.

Pine-Fresh Floor Cleaner

This formula isn't at all like the old pine solvent cleaners you may be used to. It works just as well, but leaves a light scent more reminiscent of a pine forest than a bucket of chemicals. You can adjust the scent to your preference by increasing or reducing the amount of essential oil used.

- 1 **gallon hot water**
- 2 **tablespoons liquid castile soap**
- 10 **drops pine essential oil**
- 5 **drops cypress essential oil**

Combine all ingredients in a large bucket. Dip a mop into the bucket and squeeze out excess liquid. Clean the floor by working in sections, using short strokes and dipping the mop as needed. Rinsing is not necessary.

Citrus Floor Cleaner

Nothing works like citrus in the kitchen!

- 1 **gallon hot water**
- 2 **tablespoons liquid castile soap**
- 15 **drops sweet orange essential oil**
- 8 **drops lemon essential oil, or ¼ cup lemon juice**

Combine all ingredients in a large bucket. Dip a mop into the bucket and squeeze out excess liquid. Clean the floor by working in sections, using short strokes and dipping the mop as needed. Rinsing is not necessary.

Tough Dirt & Grease Formula

Put the grease–cutting power of vinegar to use with this excellent formula.

1 gallon hot water
2 tablespoons liquid castile soap
¼ cup washing soda
1 cup vinegar
20 drops eucalyptus, peppermint, or tea tree essential oil

Combine all ingredients in a large bucket. Dip a mop into the bucket and squeeze out excess liquid. Clean the floor by working in sections, using short strokes and dipping the mop as needed. Rinsing is not necessary.

Floor Wipes

Cleaning wipes designed to fit electrostatic mops for cleaning floors have become very popular in recent years, making the traditional mop and bucket obsolete. Making your own floor wipes successfully depends on using the right materials to make the wipes from, as well as storing them properly to keep them from drying out.

To make the wipes more environmentally friendly, use cellulose cloth cut into rectangles. Cellulose is a sturdy material made from tree fibers and is free of petrochemicals. It's also completely biodegradable, unlike typical store-bought wipes. Your best bet for locating a source for this material (and, hopefully, one that makes use of a renewable tree farm) is on the Internet.

There are various ways you can store your pre-treated floor wipes — stacked in an airtight container, coiled in a can, or simply folded and sealed in a plastic bag with a zipper. Whatever option you choose, your storage container will always be reusable.

Use your homemade floor wipes on tile, linoleum, or sealed wood floors.

Rosemary-Geranium Floor Wipes

These fragrant wipes will almost make cleaning the floor a pleasure.

- 1 **cup water**
- 1 **cup white vinegar**
- 10 **drops rosemary essential oil**
- 10 **drops geranium essential oil**

Mix all ingredients in a bowl. Stack your precut wipes on top of each other (or roll them together jelly roll–style if you're going to coil the wipes to store them) and place them in the bowl with the cleaning solution. Allow the wipes to absorb the liquid for a few moments. Immediately transfer the wipes to your storage container of choice, together with about ¼ cup of the liquid to keep them moist, and seal.

The Bees Knees Floor Wipes

The botanical ingredients used in this formula will remind you of a clover-covered knoll. **Hint:** *A combination of dried red clover flowers and leaves is less expensive than buying the blossoms in bulk.*

- ½ cup water, boiled
- ½ cup red clover tea, cooled
- 1 cup white vinegar
- 10 drops grapefruit seed extract

Brew the tea by placing 2 teaspoons of the red clover into a bowl. Pour the boiled water over the herb and steep for 10 minutes, then strain. When the tea has cooled, add the remaining ingredients and blend. Soak precut wipes in this mixture for a few minutes, then store. Add just enough of the cleaning solution to the storage container to keep the wipes moist.

Helpful Hints for the Kitchen

Wipe up food spills in the oven as soon as possible. Better yet, line your oven with aluminum foil to prevent spills from caking on in the first place. Enamel stove tops can sometimes get those hard-to-wipe-off type of stains that only get worse as time goes on. But if you sprinkle on a few drops of your favorite essential oil the stain will wipe clean.

Sprinkle fresh grease spills in the oven with salt. When the oven has cooled, wipe clean with a soft cloth. Baking soda will also soak up the grease when applied this way.

Sanitize wooden cutting boards by rubbing with half of a freshly cut lemon, lime, or grapefruit. Or soak the board in a solution of 2 cups of water and 15 drops of a citrus essential oil. Then wash with a mild soap and hot water.

Electric can openers can collect a lot of gunk. Who wants to open a can of tuna for lunch after opening Fluffy and Fido's dinner the night before? Use an old, soft toothbrush dampened with 2 or 3 drops of any essential oil to clean in and between those small parts. Rinse, and the gunk is gone.

Keep garbage disposals smelling fresh by tossing in the remains of a lemon, grapefruit, or lime when available.

How about some ready-when-you-need-'em kitchen wipes? Instead of using paper towels to wipe up spills or to clean off countertops, store multiple squares of soft cotton cloth or cellulose sponge in a container filled with a mixture of 1 cup water, 1 ounce liquid castile soap, and 6 to 8 drops of your favorite essential oil. The cloths, made from old T-shirts or pajamas, can be washed and returned to the jar for reuse. Be sure to cap the jar between uses.

Keep a supply of 100 percent cotton cloths and towels on hand to use instead of paper towels.

Use cloth napkins and placemats whenever possible, to reduce your consumption of paper napkins.

Plastic storage containers can get heavily stained from foods such as tomato sauce, especially if they're frequently microwaved to reheat leftovers. For these stains, let the containers soak in a strong infusion of lemon balm, mint, or sage and a tablespoon of baking soda. After soaking for an hour or so, scrub the container with a little more baking soda if needed. The stains may not disappear entirely, but they're bound to look better than before.

Reduce your use of plastic wrap, aluminum foil, and brown paper bags by using plastic containers to tote lunches to work or school. That goes for plastic tableware as well. All are dishwasher safe; with proper care they can last for years. And plastic containers can always be used to store other materials when they are retired from kitchen service.

THE BATH

THE BATHROOM IS A BREEDING GROUND FOR GERMS, due to the nature of things we do there. Other than the obvious activities, there's also a lot of hair brushing, sloughing of dry skin, and other bodycare rituals with the potential for mold and mildew making. If you have more than one bathroom, there's more of the same going on there. These formulas are gentle on your hands and get the job done without harmful chemicals.

Mold & Mildew Busters

Mold and mildew are always a threat, especially if there is a window with a sill in your bathroom. The steam from showers and baths can affect the woodwork of the window and lead to peeling paint and mildew spots. Ventilation, such as an exhaust fan, can help minimize this problem.

The same applies to the shower curtain. The best kind of shower curtain to buy is a cloth type that can be laundered. Hang it to dry in the sun to thwart mildew and bacteria.

Herbal Disinfectant

A super disinfectant formula that's incredibly easy to make.

- 2 cups hot water
- 5 sprigs fresh thyme or 10 drops thyme essential oil
- ¼ cup borax

If using the fresh herb, bring the water to a boil and pour over the thyme sprigs in a bowl. Allow to steep for 30 minutes and then strain off liquid into a plastic spray bottle. Add borax and shake well. If using the essential oil, combine all ingredients in a plastic spray bottle and shake well. Spray on surfaces and wipe clean with a damp cloth or sponge.

Pine Disinfectant

You'll definitely prefer this recipe to your old pine cleaner!

- **2 cups water**
- **2 teaspoons borax**
- **8 drops pine essential oil**
- **4 drops cedar essential oil**

Combine all ingredients in a plastic spray
bottle. Shake before each use. Spray on
surfaces and wipe clean with a damp
cloth or sponge.

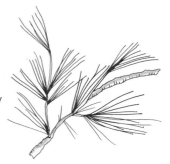

Mold & Mildew Prevention Formula

*Use this formula on shower stalls and curtains, the tracks between
sliding glass doors, and other moist areas.*

- **2   cups water**
- **8–10 drops citrus seed extract**
- **2   teaspoons tea tree essential oil**
- **4   drops juniper essential oil**

Combine all ingredients in a plastic spray bottle. Spray areas
and surfaces well but do not rinse. *Note:* If you already have a
buildup of mold or mildew, allow the spray to rest on the surface areas for a few hours. Wipe with a soft cloth, then respray
the areas and let dry without rinsing.

Mold Deterrent

If you already have a buildup of mold or mildew, allow the spray to rest on the surface areas for a few hours. Wipe with a soft cloth, then respray the areas and let dry without rinsing.

- 1¼ cups white vinegar
- ¾ cup water
- 4 drops cinnamon essential oil
- 6 drops patchouli essential oil
- 2 teaspoons tea tree essential oil

Combine all ingredients in a plastic spray bottle. Spray surfaces well but do not rinse.

MIRROR BRIGHT

This mixture not only cleans the mirror (and faucets) to a shine, but it will help to prevent fogging while the shower is running.

- 1½ cups vinegar
- ½ cup water
- 8 drops citrus oil

Combine all ingredients in a plastic spray bottle and shake well before use. Spray solution onto mirror and wipe with a dry cloth or towel.

Scouring Powders & Cleansers

The following cleaners possess sanitizing and antibacterial qualities while offering a variety of herbal scents. You can make larger batches of these products and store them in plastic containers. (Large plastic spice jars with shaker tops work great for this purpose.)

Herbal Scouring Powder for Sinks

This powder rubs out grime while leaving a fresh, earthy scent. Make sure you rinse well to remove any residue.

- 1   cup baking soda
- ¼   cup dried sage leaves, ground
- ¼   cup rosemary leaves, crushed
- 1   teaspoon cream of tartar

Combine all ingredients in a plastic container, preferably one with a shaker top. Shake well. Sprinkle a small amount of the powder into sink and scrub with a damp sponge or cloth. Rinse well with plain water.

CLEANING FAUCETS

The best things for cleaning bathroom faucets is a simple mixture of equal parts of water and vinegar. If you have a buildup of grime around the base of the faucet, put 3 or 4 drops of a citrus essential oil directly on the dirt, then clean with a toothbrush. Great for kitchen faucets, too!

Whitening Scouring Powder

The combination of borax and citrus peel will kill germs and remove stains.

- **1 cup baking soda**
- **2 teaspoons cream of tartar**
- **⅛ cup borax**
- **¼ cup grated lemon, orange, or grapefruit peel**

Combine all ingredients in a plastic container, preferably one with a shaker top. Shake well. Sprinkle a small amount of the powder into sink and scrub with a damp sponge or cloth. Rinse well.

Fragrant Scouring Powder

This formula has a clean, pleasant scent. Increase the amount of rosemary essential oil to 4 drops for more fragrance.

- **1 cup baking soda**
- **¼ cup rose petals, crushed**
- **2 drops rosemary essential oil**

Combine all ingredients in a plastic container, preferably one with a shaker top. Shake well. Sprinkle a small amount of the powder into sink and scrub with a damp sponge or cloth. Rinse well.

Lemony Scouring Powder

This formula is for lemon lovers! And with this combination of herbs, germs don't stand a chance.

- 1   **cup baking soda**
- ¼   **cup crushed, dried lemon balm leaves**
- 3   **drops lemon or lemongrass essential oil**
- 3   **drops citronella essential oil or grapefruit seed extract**

Combine all ingredients in a container, preferably one with a shaker top. Shake well. Sprinkle powder onto surface and scrub with a damp cloth or sponge. Rinse well.

Earthy Scouring Powder

This cleanser will make you think you're tending your garden instead of cleaning the bathroom. The dried rosemary leaves lend extra scrubbing action.

- 1   **cup baking soda**
- ¼   **cup dried, crushed rosemary leaves**
- 5   **drops thyme essential oil**
- 3   **drops oregano essential oil**

Combine all ingredients in a container, preferably one with a shaker top. Shake well. Sprinkle powder onto surface and scrub with a damp cloth or sponge. Rinse well.

Tub & Tile Soft Scrubber

A used plastic dishwashing liquid or shampoo bottle with a squirt top is an ideal container for your scrubber.

- **1 cup baking soda**
- **¼ cup liquid castile soap**
- **2 vitamin C tablets, crushed**
- **3–5 drops eucalyptus or tea tree essential oil**
- **water**

Combine baking soda, castile soap, vitamin C, and essential oil in a plastic bottle. Add just enough water to make a smooth liquid paste. Shake or stir to mix. Apply paste to surface and rub with a damp cloth or sponge until area is clean. Rinse several times with water.

Lavender Soft Scrubber

This scrubber not only cleans, but is mild and will actually soften your hands!

- **¾ cup baking soda**
- **¼ cup powdered milk**
- **⅛ cup liquid castile soap**
- **5 drops lavender essential oil**
- **water**

Combine baking soda, milk, castile soap, and lavender oil in a plastic squirt bottle. Add just enough water to make a smooth paste. Shake or stir to mix. Apply to surface, then wipe area clean with a damp sponge or cloth. Rinse well.

Fizzy Bathroom Sink Cleaner

Kids love to watch the "volcanic" action that occurs after pouring the vinegar over the baking soda. Who knows? You might even get your kids to clean the bathroom!

- ½   cup baking soda
- 6   drops lemon or lime essential oil
- ¼   cup vinegar

Combine the baking soda and essential oil. Sprinkle into the sink; pour the vinegar on top. After the fizz settles, scrub clean with a damp cloth or sponge. Rinse clean.

Soap Scum Remover

This formula will remove that annoying buildup that forms on soap dishes and toothbrush holders. The vinegar will produce a fizzing action.

- 1   tablespoon baking soda
- 1   teaspoon salt
- 2   drops essential oil of choice
- vinegar

Combine baking soda, salt, and essential oil in a small cup. Add just enough vinegar to make a paste. Apply to surface and scrub with a damp cloth or sponge. Rinse well.

Sanitizing the Toilet

One of the most important areas in the bathroom to clean, of course, is the commode. Most people think that the bowl itself is where the real nasties hide, but actually, it's relatively clean. Most germs take refuge behind and under the seat. Since this part is the one being handled most often, it needs careful and frequent sanitizing. There are some excellent bacteria busters offered here to do just that.

Germs-Be-Gone Toilet Cleaner

This antibacterial spray cleaner is especially formulated for cleaning the general surface area of the toilet, and under and behind the seat.

- 2 cups water
- ¼ cup liquid castile soap
- 1 tablespoon tea tree essential oil
- 10 drops eucalyptus or peppermint essential oil

Combine all ingredients in a plastic spray bottle and shake well. Spray on toilet surfaces and wipe clean with a damp cloth or sponge.

No-Scrub Toilet Bowl Cleaner

Use this one in toilet bowls that have an everlasting ring around them. (Like the kind you find in the bathroom of your vacation cabin after six months of nonuse.) You can employ this recipe just before going to bed; by morning, even the toughest of stains will have disappeared.

- **1 cup borax**
- **1 cup vinegar**
- **10 drops pine or lavender essential oil**
- **5 drops lemon or lime essential oil**

Combine all ingredients in a plastic bowl or bottle and pour all at once into the toilet bowl. Allow to sit overnight. In the morning, just flush!

Easy-Does-It Bowl Cleaner

What could be simpler than this easy and effective formula?

- **½ cup baking soda**
- **¼ cup white vinegar**
- **10 drops tea tree essential oil**

Combine all ingredients. Just add to the bowl, swipe with a brush, and you're done.

Natural Septic Care

If you have a well and septic system, you're likely aware of the importance of maintaining a healthy ecosystem of beneficial bacteria in your septic tank. Without it, organic material and paper cannot be broken down, which can result in a blockage of flow to your drain field or, worse, a backup of sewage into your home.

Household products, especially chlorinated products (such as bleach), can interfere with this natural process. Even if you use natural cleaning formulas exclusively in your home, there are still bound to be agents designed to kill bacteria going down the drain. Even running large amounts of plain water can weaken the bacterial status of a septic system.

The solution? Feed your septic tank some bacteria every 4 to 6 weeks. The best time to use these treatments is when the household is retiring for the night. That way, the treatment can get to work while people are less likely to use the bathroom.

Brown Sugar Bacteria Activator

The following formula may seem like a recipe for a bread starter, but it's actually medicine for your septic tank to help ensure a supply of beneficial bacteria to keep things flowing smoothly.

- **4   cups very warm water**
- **4   cups brown sugar**
- **2   packets active dry yeast**

Add the warm water to a large bucket, then dissolve the sugar into the water. Add the yeast and stir. Set the mixture aside for 15 to 20 minutes, or until the yeast reacts with the sugar and becomes frothy. Flush this mixture down the toilet in portions — don't try to flush it all at once.

Cornmeal Bacteria Activator

This formula utilizes the starch in cornmeal in the activation process. Incidentally, if you happen to be a home brewer, these same ingredients go into making traditional moonshine!

- **4   cups very warm water**
- **2   cups cornmeal**
- **2   cups white sugar**
- **2   packages active dry yeast**

Using a large bucket, stir the cornmeal into the warm water. Add the sugar, stirring to dissolve. Add the yeast and stir again. Set aside until the yeast becomes activated (about 15 minutes), then flush the mixture down the toilet a little at a time.

Helpful Hints for the Bathroom

To maintain a fresh scent in the bathroom, place a few drops of your favorite essential oil on the cardboard tube supporting the toilet paper. Every time the paper is used, the fragrance will be released.

Place a bowl of potpourri on the sink or toilet tank. Replace the potpourri every three months. For recipes, see chapter 8. Potpourri, whether made from natural or synthetic materials, can be toxic to pets and young children who might be tempted to handle or even eat it. If this scenario is a possibility in your home, you can place the potpourri on a high shelf. Or try filling a muslin or cloth bag with the potpourri, then hang it out of reach.

To keep bath mats and rugs smelling fresh between washings, simply scent ½ cup baking soda with 8 to 10 drops of the essential oil of your choice. Sprinkle on the carpets, wait 15 minutes, and then vacuum.

If you have a stand-alone toothbrush holder, be sure to run it through the dishwasher often. You'd be amazed at the germs and dirt that thrive there. If it's really full of gunk, let it stand for

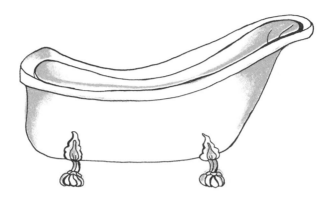

20 minutes filled with water and two or three drops of tea tree essential oil. Then wash by hand or in the dishwasher.

Don't forget to periodically clean combs and hairbrushes. Let them stand for 20 minutes in a container with 1½ cups water, ½ cup vinegar, and 20 drops of tea tree, rosemary, lavender, or eucalyptus essential oil. Rinse well and allow to air-dry before putting them away.

THE LAUNDRY

MANUFACTURERS OF LAUNDRY PRODUCTS spend a good deal of money on advertising to convince us that their products contain "magical" ingredients that can solve every laundry problem. Well, they don't. With their cleaning power stemming from caustic bleach, EDTA, and optical brighteners (which are strong allergens), their ingredients are anything but magical. But the fact is, many commercial laundry soaps contain nearly 70 percent ordinary washing soda. The difference between them basically comes down to fragrance, color, and variations in the amount of additives.

Simple Laundry Guidelines

Before you can properly clean your dirty laundry, you need to consider what you want your washer and detergent to accomplish. It doesn't do any good to wash heavily soiled work clothes with the baby's pajamas, as oils can transfer from one to the other. Likewise, you can't expect your white shirt to easily free itself of a coffee stain if you're going to wait three days before washing it. So before you even lift the lid of the washer, there are some basic laundry guidelines to follow to help preserve your garments and keep them looking their best.

Sorting Laundry

Your mother probably told you never to wash colored clothes with white ones. But she might not have told you that there's a lot more to sorting laundry. Here are some considerations when sorting:

The first step is to sort by color. Whites, very bright colors (such as red or orange), pastels, and dark colors should be washed separately. Next, sort heavy fabrics from delicate garments that must be laundered in the gentle cycle.

Towels, sheets, and bedspreads should be washed separately because they produce lint that will adhere to other fabrics, such as knits.

Don't forget to check the pockets of your children's jeans, jackets, and shirts! I've been surprised many times by the array of trinkets a child can collect in his pockets, including coins and partially eaten foodstuffs. On one memorable occasion, a broken ballpoint pen remained undetected until it had been through the dryer! (Although the inside of the dryer ended up with a polka-dot pattern, the ink wiped away easily with a rag moistened with vinegar and cedar essential oil.)

Before You Wash

Pretreating is all-important if you really want to rid your clothes of stains and heavy soiling. These are the best stain-fighting tactics:

Follow this golden rule of the laundry room: pretreat stains as soon as possible. Always rinse a stain in cold water — warm water can cause fruit and sugar stains to set in. See page 82–84 for pretreatment formulas.

Prewash heavily soiled items to help eliminate most of the dirt without redepositing it on clothes. After running clothes through the prewash cycle, drain and wash in the regular cycle — in hot water if the fabric permits it.

Presoak old or tough stains like blood and grass for 30 minutes or more.

Water Temperature

Your washing machine comes equipped with a water temperature control for a reason: not all fabrics are created equal. Always follow specific instructions given on a garment's care label. To avoid damaging garments, remember:

Washing in cold water will prevent shrinking and the release of dyes. Bright colors, lightly soiled items, and delicate garments should be washed in cold water. Rinsing in cold water is suitable for all types of laundry. And you'll be saving energy, too.

Warm water helps to reduce wrinkling and the bleeding of colors. Choose warm water washing for permanent press, washable wool, dark colors, and synthetic fabrics.

Hot water is recommended for heavily soiled clothing, towels, whites, pastels, and light-colored prints. Never wash 100 percent cotton or 100 percent wool items in hot water or they will shrink. Instead, use cold water for cotton and hand wash wool items.

The Detergent Dilemma

Believe it or not, you're probably using more laundry product than you need per load. How much do you really need to use? The usual recommended capful is almost twice as much as you need for an average load. In fact, excess detergent leads to residue that only traps dirt in the clothes you've just washed. It's not only environmentally friendly to use less, it's easier on your clothing and your budget, too.

Here are some other detergent tips:

Keep a big jug of white vinegar in your laundry area. It makes blankets soft and fluffy and dissolves uric acid, making it perfect for washing babies' items. Vinegar also reduces soap residue, breaks up grease and oil, and is a natural bleach. As an added benefit, washing clothes in vinegar can help prevent static cling in the dryer.

Laundry soap doesn't perform as well in hard water, but this can be corrected by adding zeolite powder, orrisroot, baking soda, or borax to the wash.

Wondering where to find soap flakes? Ivory Snow was the answer for decades, but the formula changed in 1991, and it became a detergent. For many years afterward, soap flakes were not commercially available, leaving only one other option: grating a bar of natural soap to use in recipes. Now pure soap flakes are again on the market! Soaps Gone Buy sells heavy-duty grated laundry soap in 2-pound bags, and Dri-Pak Soap Flakes, sold in either

1-pound bags or 1-pound boxes, is made in England and imported by MSO Distributing (see Resources). They're easy to use and unscented. You can still grate your own flakes — and if you are a soapmaker, grating soap for these recipes is a great way to use misshapen bars you don't want to give as gifts.

The Herbal Touch

Herbal essential oils can be blended into laundry formulas (liquid or powder) or added to the softener dispenser of your machine. Essential oils not only boost cleaning power, they also provide a fresh, clean scent.

Essential oils can also lend therapeutic qualities. For instance, add tea tree essential oil to your laundry if you suffer from frequent yeast infections. Eucalyptus essential oil can be used when someone in the household is fighting a cold. Jasmine, rose, or ylang-ylang essential oil will impart a romantic scent to fine washables. You are encouraged to experiment! You can even create your own unique blend from the essential oil chart on the following page.

Herbal-scented baking soda is another way to use essential oils in the laundry. Baking soda adds whitening power and is a natural water softener. For a 16-ounce box, use 15 to 20 drops of essential oil.

You can mix it right in the box! Simply add the oils to the box and shake well. Or add 3 to 5 drops of essential oil to 1 cup of white vinegar; the oil lends additional cleaning power and helps to remove odors.

Be creative in your thinking, and you'll soon find that you don't miss store-bought detergents at all.

Essential Oil Chart for Laundry

All of these essential oils help clean and freshen the laundry. They offer other benefits as well.

HERB	PROPERTIES
Cedar	Adds a clean, woodsy scent
Chamomile	Soothing
Eucalyptus	Excellent for colds and sinus trouble
Lavender	Relaxing
Lemon	Stimulating, helps whiten laundry
Peppermint	Good for colds and sinus trouble
Rose geranium	Adds a romantic scent
Rosemary*	Calming (but often stimulating on its own)
Sweet orange	Helps remove stains and whiten laundry
Tea tree	Antibacterial and antifungal

*Not suitable for wool, silk, or satin

Making Natural Laundry Soaps

These formulas don't have any magical components that you can't pronounce. Instead, the cleaning power of these soaps comes from combining clean, pure ingredients.

Basic Liquid Formula

Dr. Bronner's, one of the most popular liquid castile soaps, is available in a variety of scents today, if you wish to skip adding your own essential oils.

- **2¼ cups liquid castile soap**
- **¼ cup white distilled vinegar**
- **1 tablespoon glycerin**
- **¾ cup water**
- **10–15 drops essential oil of your choice**

Combine all ingredients into a plastic container or squirt bottle. Shake once or twice before adding to the wash. To use, add ¼ cup per average load; ½ cup for extra large or heavily soiled loads.

Basic Laundry Soap Powder

This recipe will wash six average loads, but you can easily double it.

- 1   cup washing soda
- 1   cup scented baking soda (see essential oil chart for selection)
- 1   cup soap flakes or finely grated pure bar soap

Combine all ingredients and store in a heavy plastic container. Use ½ cup for an average laundry load.

Lemon Fresh Linen Wash

This formula can be used for any type of laundry, but it's especially nice for cotton linens that have been allowed to dry naturally in the sun after washing. The aloe vera juice and vinegar soften, while citric acid and grapefruit extract brighten and sanitize.

- 2   cups liquid castile soap
- ½   cup aloe vera juice
- ½   cup white vinegar
- 1   cup water
- 1   tablespoon powdered citric acid
- 2   teaspoons grapefruit seed extract
- 15–20 drops lemon (or lemongrass) essential oil

Combine all ingredients into a plastic container, preferably one with a pour spout. Give this formula a gentle shake, or just turn it upside down once or twice to make sure all of the ingredients are evenly distributed before adding it to the washing machine. For an average load, use ¼ cup.

Hard Water Formula

Hard water can affect the performance of your laundry soap. This formula uses borax and vinegar as natural water softeners.

- **1** **cup soap flakes or finely grated pure bar soap**
- **1** **cup washing soda**
- **½** **cup borax**
- **2** **cups vinegar**
- **10** **drops essential oil of choice**

Combine the soap, washing soda, and borax in a heavy plastic container. Blend the vinegar and essential oils in a separate container, preferably one with a pour spout. Use ½ cup of the soap mixture for washing; add ½ cup of the vinegar mixture during the rinse cycle.

Fine Washables Formula

Rosemary is an old favorite for freshening delicate knits and lingerie. Note: *Do not use on items that are 100 percent wool, silk, or satin.*

- **1** **ounce liquid castile soap**
- **1** **cup rosemary infusion**

Steep two sprigs of fresh, bruised rosemary (slightly crushed between the fingers to release the oils), or steep 1 teaspoon of dried, crushed rosemary leaves in 1 cup boiling water for 15 minutes, then strain. If using essential oil, add 3 drops to 1 cup of hot water. Place the clothes in the washer and add the castile soap and rosemary infusion. Launder in cold water on the gentle cycle.

Baby's Laundry Formula

Babies can sure get their clothing messy! Borax and vinegar will help to whiten and soften fabrics.

- **2** drops essential oil (optional)
- **2** tablespoons liquid castile soap
- **¼** cup washing soda
- **1** cup baking soda
- **¼** cup borax
- **¼** cup white vinegar

If using essential oil, mix with the castile soap. Add this mixture to washer along with the washing soda, baking soda, borax, and vinegar. Launder as usual.

DIAPER WHITENER

Add ½ cup borax, ½ cup vinegar, and 6 to 8 drops of essential oil to a pail or bucket of hot water. Soak diapers for 20 to 30 minutes, or more if heavily soiled, before laundering.

Bright Colors Formula

This recipe makes enough for one load. You can make larger batches, but keep the liquid castile soap separate.

> 1   ounce liquid castile soap (scented with 2 to 4 drops essential oil, if desired)
> ¼   cup washing soda
> ½   cup Epsom salts

Add the liquid castile soap to washer, then add washing soda and Epsom salts. Launder as usual.

Bleach Alternative Formula

This formula makes enough for one load of laundry. You can make larger batches, but keep the lemon juice mixture separate until ready to use.

> ½   cup Basic Liquid Formula (page 77)
> ¼   cup borax
> ¼   cup lemon juice or vinegar, plus 6 drops lemon essential oil

Combine all ingredients in a heavy plastic jug or other container of choice. For extra whitening power, let the clean clothes hang outside to dry in the sun.

Natural Fabrics Rescue

Natural fabrics, such as wool and silk, need special care. Wool should be hand washed in cool water and a capful of liquid castile soap, then rinsed well in a tub of clean water. Never allow wool to soak. Nor should you attempt to wring wool dry. After the final rinse, place the wool garment on a dry towel and roll up like a jelly roll. Gently press on the towel to remove excess water. Repeat this process if necessary with another towel. Then place the garment flat on a dry towel, reshape, and leave it to dry.

Silk items should be dipped in a solution of warm water and a capful of liquid castile soap. Rinse well and gently squeeze out excess water. Turn the garment inside out and hang until it is just damp to the touch. With the garment still reversed, press with an iron on low setting.

Pretreatments for Stains

Since vinegar can remove some dyes, test these formulas on a small area of the fabric before treating the actual stain.

Tea Tree & Salt Presoak

This stain remover is another great vinegar-based solution.

> 1   cup vinegar
> ½   cup salt
> 3   drops tea tree essential oil

Place clothes in washer and add enough warm water to cover them. Combine all ingredients and add to washer. Let clothes soak for an hour or more, then wash as usual.

Perspiration Stain Remover

Use this formula to pretreat ring around the collar and perspiration stains.

- ¼ cup vinegar
- 4 drops lemon, lime, or eucalyptus essential oil
- 1 tablespoon baking soda

Combine all ingredients. Rub the mixture into the stains with your fingers, a soft cloth, or an old toothbrush. Launder as usual.

Lemon & Tea Tree Perspiration Presoak

Try this fresh-smelling pretreatment before you wash.

- 1 cup vinegar
- ¼ cup lemon juice
- 6 drops tea tree essential oil

Combine all ingredients and add to the clothes in a washer full of warm water. Allow to soak for an hour or two, then wash as usual.

All-Purpose Stain Spray

Since food and drink spills aren't likely to occur while you're in the laundry room, why not make up extra bottles and keep this formula handy in the kitchen and bath as well?

¼ cup vegetable oil–based soap

¼ cup glycerin

2 tablespoons borax

10 drops peppermint or tea tree essential oil

1¾ cups water

Combine all ingredients in a plastic spray bottle and shake well. Spray generously onto stain. Launder as usual.

On-the-Spot Stain Lifter

Accidents happen, but this stain remover will make you forget the stain was ever there.

2 tablespoons cream of tartar

2 drops peppermint, eucalyptus, or lemon essential oil

water

Combine all ingredients in a small cup, using just enough water to make a paste. Spread the paste over the stain and allow it to dry completely before washing.

Tricks for Wool & Silk

Sometimes, a small stain is all that stands between your wearing a wool jacket or silk blouse out again and wearing it out completely with frequent cleanings. This simple spot treatment can help remove unsightly stains without cleaning the entire garment. This treatment can be used on most fabrics (including wool or silk), but don't try this on rayon.

The method: Moisten a cotton ball with white vinegar, being careful to avoid saturation. Gently dab the cotton ball onto the stain, but don't rub. Let the vinegar work for a minute or two. Then blot the stain with a dry, clean cloth several times.

Baby Your Silk

Since silk is a protein fiber, it cannot withstand coming into contact with soap that has a pH of 10 or higher. Like human hair, silk fibers have a natural coating of oils that must be preserved to stay looking good. In fact, this coating helps the material to resist dirt and stains. Gentle hand washing is the best way to avoid risking damage to silk from high alkali agents and the agitator of the washing machine.

Combine 1 capful low pH castile soap (such as Dr. Bronner's Aloe Vera Baby-Mild Castile Soap) in a small tub or basin full of cool or lukewarm water, swirling with your hand to distribute the soap. Place the silk garment into the water and gently dip it up and down several times (you mustn't allow silk to soak). Rinse thoroughly in cool or lukewarm water (never hot!), but don't wring or twist the garment. Lay the garment flat on some towels and, using your hands, press the excess water out. Then let the item hang dry.

REVIVE FADED OR YELLOWED SILK
Hand wash as described above, but add one of the following to the wash water: ¼ cup hydrogen peroxide; ¼ cup white vinegar; or 15 drops tea tree oil diluted into a ¼ cup cool water. Follow the directions above for rinsing and drying the silk garment.

Be Cool with Wool

You can hand wash wool items in the same manner as described above for silk garments, except you should gently squeeze the wool garment while washing, don't dip. Also, do *not* hang wool to dry. Instead, it must be allowed to dry on a flat surface.

Laundry Problem-Solvers

Sometimes, real life happens and we can't always tend to a stain right away. Or the stain is the worst you can ask for, such as red wine, blood, or ink. But before you toss the garment out or make it into a dusting cloth, give one of these natural remedies a try. If a stain doesn't come out the first time, it's worth repeating the process. Whatever you do, don't put the garment into the dryer if the stain is still visible after air-drying; doing so could make the stain permanent.

The following is a list of the most troublesome types of stains and some suggested remedies. Some of these stain problem-solvers involve herbal teas or extracts, while some call for other easy-to-use natural ingredients that you probably have on hand.

Baby formula. Anyone who has cared for an infant knows that formula, especially those that are soy-based, makes an ugly stain. But if formula stains are treated when they land on clothing, they can sometimes leave a ring after laundering. To treat them, rub a mixture of vinegar and a few drops of garlic juice into the stain. This will help to break down the protein in the formula and release it from the fabric. A little moistened meat tenderizer will do the same thing. I also discovered long ago that baby wipes — which are basically a combination of alcohol, mild cleanser, and emollients — will remove these stains beautifully if applied right away, and are safe for most fabrics. Choose the method best for the age of the stain and the type of fabric that you're treating.

Berries. If the stain is fresh, rub a slice of lemon over it several times. If the stain is old, treat it with glycerin and wait 30 minutes. Rinse and allow to air-dry. If the stain endures, make a mixture of 1 heaping tablespoon cornstarch, 2 drops eucalyptus essential oil, and 1 teaspoon glycerin. Add just enough water to make a thick paste and spread on the stain. Without rinsing, put the garment in the sun to dry. Repeat the paste application if necessary. Once the stain is gone you can launder as usual.

Blood. Immediately rinse the garment thoroughly in cool water. If necessary, let the garment soak in a solution of laundry soap and water for several hours. For light-colored fabrics, try wiping with a soft cloth moistened with hydrogen peroxide. Hang the garment in the sun and keep applying hydrogen peroxide until all traces of the stain are gone. Allow to dry and launder as usual.

Butter or margarine. Make a paste of 1 tablespoon baking soda; 2 drops lemon, lime, or orange essential oil; and water. Spread the paste on the stain and allow to dry, then wash as usual.

Candle wax. First harden the wax with ice cubes and gently peel off as much as you can. Then place the stained area between paper towels and press with a warm iron. Keep moving or replacing the paper towels to avoid transferring the candle wax back into the fabric. Continue this procedure until the paper towels no longer absorb the wax. The remaining stain should then be treated with a little glycerin on a cotton ball and laundered as usual.

Chewing gum. If chewing gum makes its way onto clothing, put the garment in a plastic bag and place in the freezer for 30 to 45 minutes. The gum should pull right off. If a residue remains, soak in full-strength vinegar before washing.

Chocolate. Make a paste of borax and water and spread over the stain. Allow to dry and then launder as usual.

Coffee and tea. Immediately flush with cool water. Then soak in a borax and water solution before laundering.

Egg. Scrape off any dried material. Douse the remaining stain with a mixture of 2 teaspoons lemon juice and 3 drops sweet orange or lemon essential oil. Wash in cold water.

Grass. Soak garment in vinegar, then spread a paste of baking soda and water over the stain. Wash in hot water.

Grease. Cover the stain with a mixture of 2 teaspoons each of cornmeal, salt, and baking soda. Let this mixture stand for 30 minutes or more to absorb as much grease as possible, then wipe away. Soak the remaining stain in ½ cup vinegar, 5 drops lemon or orange essential oil or grapefruit seed extract, and ¼ cup water until the stain breaks free. If the fabric can tolerate it, wash in hot water.

Ink. Place a cloth under the fabric and dab the stain repeatedly with undiluted eucalyptus essential oil until it begins to break up. The ink will begin to transfer to the underlying cloth. Remove as much of the stain as you can with this method. Then soak the garment in a solution of equal parts of vinegar and milk before washing.

Linens. Linens can sometimes yellow if stored in a trunk or closet for a long time. The best prevention is to wrap them carefully in acid-free paper before storing. If yellowing does occur you can soak them in a tea made from 2 or 3 fresh rhubarb stalks and 3 cups boiling water. Allow the material to dry in the sun. Repeat as necessary until the stains have disappeared. You can also use 1 cup lemon juice diluted in 2 cups water in place of the rhubarb tea.

Lipstick. Gently massage the stain with white toothpaste or 3 to 4 drops of glycerin for a few minutes and blot dry. Then wipe several times with eucalyptus essential oil. Launder as usual. Repeat the eucalyptus application if the stain doesn't come out completely after washing.

Mold and mildew. Sometimes towels are left in a duffel bag after a day at the beach, or clothes are put into storage while still damp, resulting in mold or mildew stains. Pretreat these stains with a solution of ¼ cup vinegar, 1 teaspoon salt, and 6 drops tea tree essential oil. Launder as usual.

Mustard. Mustard contains turmeric, which yields a bright yellow dye. To break up the stain, apply some glycerin and let stand for 30 minutes.

Then gently massage some laundry soap (liquid or powder) into the stain and wash as usual.

Nail polish. First try blotting the stain with rubbing alcohol. If this doesn't work, test some nail polish remover in an inconspicuous place on the garment. If the test area of the fabric isn't damaged, proceed to the stain. *Note:* Organic nail polish removers are available at health food stores that carry natural cosmetics.

Oil. Carefully blot up excess oil from the garment, then follow the treatment recommended for grease stains.

Paint. Success depends on the type of paint involved. Latex paint is easily removed by rinsing in hot soapy water. Oil-based paint is another matter, and your best chance is to act immediately. Rub the stain with rubbing alcohol, then soak in a solution of equal parts hot vinegar and milk for several hours. If this doesn't work, you may have to take the garment to a professional cleaner or accept the fact that it's now a dust cloth.

Pencil. Pencil marks may seem innocent, but they can persist after washing. The cure is simple: Rub them off with an eraser before washing.

Rust. Make a paste of lemon juice and salt. Let the paste sit on the stain for several minutes and then pour boiling water over the stain. Or, boil the garment in 1 tablespoon cream of tartar and 1 quart of water. An old-fashioned but time-tested remedy for rust stains is to let the fabric soak in a cooled infusion made from 2 to 3 fresh rhubarb stalks and 3 cups boiling water.

Salad dressing. Soak in a solution of ½ cup vinegar, ½ cup lemon juice, and 6 to 8 drops of sweet orange, eucalyptus, or tea tree essential oil for 30 minutes. Then launder as usual, in hot water if the fabric permits it.

Scorch marks. For light-colored fabrics, test a small area with hydrogen peroxide. If no damage occurs, treat the stain by dabbing on hydrogen peroxide, then hang the garment in direct sunlight. Keep the stain moistened with additional hydrogen peroxide until the scorch marks fade. For darker clothing, coat the stain with glycerin and allow to rest overnight. Then wash as usual. If any residue from the glycerin remains after washing, it can be removed by rubbing with liquid castile soap and rinsing thoroughly.

Shoe polish. Water or any other wet treatment will cause this stain to spread. Instead, blot the stain with glycerin on a soft, clean cloth to loosen it from the garment's fibers, then launder as usual.

Tar. Fresh tar can be countered by first scraping off surface pieces with a warm butter knife. Dried tar should first be treated with glycerin or olive oil to soften it. Then place the garment over several folded paper towels and pour on 2 or 3 drops of eucalyptus essential oil. The paper towels will absorb the dissolving tar underneath, so replace them as needed. Keep working with the knife during this process to scrape off the lifting tar. Repeat this process until the tar has been removed.

Urine. Soak the material in a solution of 1 cup vinegar, 5 drops lavender essential oil, and, if the fabric can tolerate it, 1 cup very hot water for 30 minutes. Then wash as usual.

Wine. Rinse in cool water right away, then follow the procedure for removing berry stains.

Fabric Softeners

Vinegar is the fabric softener of choice for many reasons. Not only is it nontoxic, it also removes soap residue in the rinse cycle and helps to prevent static cling in the dryer. The fun part is in using different scented vinegars. Essential oils can produce a fresh, clean, floral, woodsy, or spicy effect — use whatever fragrance suits your fancy.

Adding one or two cups of vinegar to the rinse cycle is fine for whites, but more than that can cause some dyes to run, especially from rayon fabrics. Keep the color and fabric in mind when using these formulas.

Lavender Fabric Softener

Formulas don't get much easier than this one, which is both fragrant and effective.

- **1 gallon vinegar**
- **20 drops lavender essential oil**

Add the lavender essential oil to the vinegar right in the container and you've got instant fabric softener! Shake well before using. For a large load, add 1 cup during the rinse cycle; use ½ cup during the rinse cycle for smaller loads.

Orange Glow Fabric Softener

White vinegar softens hard water and reduces static cling. The addition of sweet orange essential oil provides a fresh, clean scent.

- 8 cups water
- 6 cups white vinegar
- 1 cup baking soda
- 25 drops sweet orange essential oil

Combine all ingredients in a large plastic jug. Shake well before adding ½ cup to the rinse cycle.

Minty-Fresh Fabric Softener

This formula helps remove tough odors from clothing.

- 1 gallon vinegar
- 10 drops peppermint essential oil

Combine ingredients in a heavy-duty plastic container. Add 1 cup to the rinse cycle for each load.

Lemony Fabric Softener

There's nothing like the smell of lemons to suggest freshness.

- 6 cups vinegar
- 1 cup water
- 1 cup baking soda
- 15 drops lemon or lemongrass essential oil

Combine all ingredients in a heavy-duty plastic container. Add 1 cup to the rinse cycle for each load for truly lemon-fresh clothes.

DRYER SHEETS

This idea is clever and simple — natural dryer sheets can be made from a scrap of cotton cloth and 3 to 5 drops of your favorite essential oil. Using more may actually soil your newly washed laundry. Here are some interesting combinations you could try:

* Cedar and patchouli for a masculine, woodsy scent
* Rosemary and thyme for an earthy scent
* Geranium and neroli (orange blossom) for a floral scent
* Peppermint and eucalyptus for cold sufferers
* Jasmine and ylang ylang for a romantic scent
* Sweet orange and lemon for a refreshing scent
* Chamomile and hyssop for a relaxing effect (helps insomnia!)

Cut a scrap of cotton cloth into a small square (about 4 inches), and add 3 to 5 drops of your favorite essential oil. Toss into the dryer with the rest of the laundry. You can use the same cloth two or three times, each time refreshing it with 3 more drops essential oil. After that, wash the cloth and it's ready to be used again.

Natural Moth Repellents

When it comes time to store your wool sweaters and coats, you'll want to keep moths away so you'll find your garments in one piece the following season. Aside from the terrible smell that regular mothballs give off (which seeps into clothing), they contain paradichlorobenzene, which is very toxic. The following alternatives are safe and just as effective.

Tuck away sachets of cedar chips with your wool items.

If storing your items in a trunk or other container, place a tea towel or a sheet of tissue paper that has been sprinkled with several drops of lavender and rosemary essential oils on top.

If your clothing will be hanging, also hang a few whole, dried lemon peels in the closet where the clothing will be stored.

Lavender Linen Drawer Liners

Keeping lingerie and clothing fresh couldn't be easier with this fragrant idea. When the lavender flowers have lost their scent, simply open the fabric pocket and replace the flower buds with fresh ones.

1   cup dried lavender flowers
cotton or linen fabric to line drawers
Velcro (the kind with the sticky backing)

1. Cut two pieces of fabric of equal size that will fit snugly on the inside of the drawer you wish to line. Press the sticky backed Velcro around the edge of each piece of fabric so that the pieces will stick to each other when pressed together.

2. Spread the dried lavender flowers in an even layer on one piece of the fabric with the Velcro facing up. Place the other precut fabric on top, Velcro facing down. Press down on the fabric to form a pocket and seal from the Velcro edging.

Geranium Gift Wrap Closet Liners

Make use of leftover gift wrap and keep towels and linens smelling sweet at the same time. You can also use this lining in bathroom drawers, or kitchen cupboards and pantries.

> **gift wrap**
> **geranium essential oil**

Measure the shelf or drawer that you'll be lining so you can cut the gift wrap to the right size. After cutting, smooth out the gift wrap on a table, printed side down. Moisten a cotton ball with 5–6 drops of the geranium essential oil and rub it lengthwise across the paper. Line the closet shelf (or drawer) with the scented gift wrap, scented side down. *Note:* To keep the lining from slipping, use a staple gun to secure the corner edges to the shelf. This makes removal of the liner much easier than using tape or glue.

LAUNDRY STARCH

Here's a quick alternative to the commercial, chemical-laden starches.

- 1 cup water
- 2 tablespoons cornstarch
- 2 drops of essential oil of choice (for light colors, use a clear oil like tea tree)
- ½ cup cooled black tea (for dark colors only)

Combine all ingredients in a plastic spray bottle. Shake well before each use. Lightly spray the garment and iron as usual.

WOOD CARE

IT ISN'T NECESSARY TO USE AN OILY PRODUCT every time you dust your furniture. In fact, some types of furniture never need oil, just a dusting with a damp cloth. Some older pieces and unfinished wood, however, can benefit from an occasional oil treatment.

It's the same story with hardwood flooring — some floors are given a surface finish and others a penetrating finish. If your hardwood floor has a shiny, glossy appearance, it probably has a coating of varnish, such as polyurethane. For this type of flooring, regular cleaning with a vegetable-oil wood soap will remove any surface dirt and restore a high sheen. If your floor doesn't come back to life after cleaning, it may need a new surface finish. If your floor has a slightly oily feel when you draw your hand across it, it likely has a penetrating finish and needs additional waxing now and then to protect it.

Wood Cleaners

These formulas are for furniture with a hard finish and in need of a good surface cleaning, like garage and estate sale finds, or items kept in storage for a long time. If cleaning the wood doesn't revive the piece, it may be time for refinishing.

Fragrant Wood Cleaner

This fragrant formula will clear away sticky grime. Using bergamot or geranium essential oil will give a floral scent.

- ½ cup lemon juice
- 1 teaspoon liquid castile soap
- 4 drops bergamot, geranium, or sweet orange essential oil

Combine all ingredients in a small plastic spray bottle. Apply to wood and wipe clean with a damp cloth. Wipe again with a dry cloth.

BE WOOD WARY

Always test wood cleaning formulas on an inconspicuous area of your furniture, like the inside of a leg or a panel underneath, before treating the entire piece. This step is a very important one, as some essential oils can adversely affect certain wood finishes.

Berry Good for Wood Cleaner

Use this fruity solution to bring dingy, dull wood furniture back to life.

- 1 **tablespoon fresh raspberry leaves**
- 1 **cup boiling water**
- ½ **cup vinegar**
- ½ **cup lemon juice**

Steep raspberry leaves in water for 20 minutes. Strain. In a plastic spray bottle, combine tea, vinegar, and lemon juice. Shake well. Moisten a soft cloth with the solution and gently rub the wood to loosen and remove dirt. Use a second clean cloth dampened with water to remove any residue. Wipe again with a dry towel.

Dusting Aids

These formulas are useful for regular dusting, and they smell great, too. Choose one that's right for the type of wood you have.

Lemon-Fresh Dust Buster

This recipe is for a single use. You could make larger quantities, but the presence of lemon juice necessitates refrigeration. If you want to make enough to store in a plastic spray bottle, you could increase the amount of lemon balm tea to 2 cups, omit the lemon juice, and increase the lemon essential oil to 20 drops.

- ¼ cup lemon juice
- ⅛ cup cooled lemon balm tea
- 2 drops thyme essential oil
- 4 drops lemon essential oil

Combine all ingredients in a plastic spray bottle and shake well. Spray onto wood and wipe clean with a dry cloth.

Cedarwood Dusting Aid

Here's my personal favorite! I use it for bookcases, coffee tables, kitchen cabinets, and the antique dining room table that we refinished a few years back. I adore the scent of cedar on wood; the sweet orange oil adds just the right touch. This recipe makes enough for a large plastic spray bottle.

- ½ cup oil soap (I like Murphy's Oil Soap)
- ¾ cup water
- 5 drops sweet orange or patchouli essential oil
- 15–20 drops cedar essential oil

Combine all ingredients in a plastic spray bottle and shake well. Spray onto wood and wipe clean with a soft, dry cloth.

Moisture-Rich Duster

This recipe is nourishing for older, dry wood. But use it sparingly as too much oil left on the wood will attract more dust. Adjust the amount of linseed and essential oils needed based on how much surface area you are treating.

- scant ⅛ cup linseed oil
- 3 drops lemon or sweet orange essential oil

Combine ingredients in a small cup and stir to mix. Apply small amounts at a time to a dry cloth and rub well into wood. Wipe with a dry cloth to remove any oil residue.

Wood Polishes, Washes & Waxes

You can make larger batches of any of these formulas and store in a recycled coffee can or glass jar with a screw-top lid. Just be sure to shake or stir before applying to the polishing cloth. Keeping an old toothbrush or small paintbrush in the can or jar is an easy and less messy way of getting the liquid polish onto the cloth.

Herbal Wood Polish

This formula leaves a light herbal aroma.

- ¼ cup linseed oil
- 3 drops lavender or rosemary essential oil

Combine oils in a bowl. Apply a light layer of polish to wood with a brush or cloth. Rub into wood with a soft cloth, using circular motions. Wipe again with a dry cloth.

Lemon-Walnut Wood Polish

If making a larger quantity to store, use 15 drops lemon essential oil instead of the lemon juice.

- ⅛ cup walnut oil
- ⅛ cup linseed oil
- ¼ cup lemon juice

Combine all ingredients in a bowl (or clean coffee can with lid, if making in quantity). Apply a light layer of polish to wood with a brush or cloth. Rub into wood with a soft cloth, using circular motions. Wipe again with a dry cloth.

Carnauba & Lavender Wood Paste

Carnauba is the hardest wax available. Combined with oil, it is an excellent wood restorative.

- **2 tablespoons carnauba wax chips**
- **1 cup linseed, almond, walnut, or olive oil**
- **6 drops lavender essential oil**

1. Combine carnauba and linseed oil in a double boiler. Heat slowly, stirring until completely melted.
2. Remove from heat, add essential oil, and blend well. Pour into a glass or tin container and allow to cool completely before sealing.
3. To use, spread the paste on wood with a soft, dry cloth using small, circular motions. Buff with a second dry cloth.

FURNITURE FIX

If grease is spilled or splattered on wooden furniture, immediately cover the stain with salt to absorb as much grease as possible. Wait an hour and then vacuum or carefully brush away the salt with a dry cloth.

If a grease stain remains, put a soft towel over the spot and press with a warm iron — but be careful not to scorch the wood! Keep shifting the towel around, or replace it with a fresh one to avoid redepositing grease on the wood.

Traditional Beeswax Polish

This formula is used on quality wood pieces (especially antique furniture) that have been treated with a light penetrating finish; do not use on lacquered, painted, or unfinished surfaces. The formula calls for turpentine, but you can substitute a citrus peel–derived product called Plant Thinner, made by Auro Organics (available in some health food stores). If using turpentine, take extra care in handling and storing.

- 8 ounces unrefined beeswax, grated
- 2½ cups turpentine
- 2 cups water
- ½ cup lemon juice
- 2 ounces grated castile soap
- 15 drops essential oil of choice

1. Melt the beeswax slowly in a double boiler. When melted, remove from heat and carefully stir in the turpentine. Set aside.

2. In a medium saucepan, bring the water and lemon juice to a boil. Add the castile soap and stir until the soap melts. Allow this mixture to cool for 5 minutes.

3. Very slowly, pour the lemon juice mixture in a fine stream into the beeswax mixture, stirring constantly. Add the essential oil and blend well. Pour into a shallow glass jar or tin can and allow to cool completely before putting the lid on.

4. Dip a soft, dry cloth into the polish and spread a small amount on the wood surface; use small, circular motions. Wipe and buff with a second dry cloth.

Hardwood Floor Wash

If you have loose boards or wood tiles, hand wipe these areas with the wash. Excess liquid from the mop can get in the cracks and cause further buckling.

- **1½ cups water**
- **1½ cups vinegar**
- **20 drops peppermint essential oil**

Combine all ingredients in a plastic spray bottle. Use sparingly, working on small sections of the floor. Dry mop the floor after washing.

Double-Nut Wood Polish

This one smells almost good enough to eat! (But don't.)

- **¼ cup almond oil**
- **⅛ cup walnut oil**
- **4 drops pure vanilla extract**

Combine all ingredients in a bowl. Apply a light layer of polish to wood with a brush or cloth. Rub into wood with a soft cloth, using circular motions. Wipe again with a dry cloth.

WOOD PANELING

Most wood paneling can be damaged by the application of liquids and only requires occasional dusting with a soft cloth. If it has an oily finish, however, you can mist the cloth with a cleaner such as Cedarwood Dusting Aid (see page 105) or an oily cleaner such as Moisture-Rich Duster (see page 105). As with flooring or wood furniture, test the formula on a small area first.

Citrus-Scented Wood Floor Wax

In this formula, the lemon juice and essential oils clean while the beeswax and carnauba wax nourish.

- 1 **cup linseed oil**
- ¼ **cup lemon juice**
- 2 **tablespoons grated beeswax**
- 2 **tablespoons carnauba wax**
- 6 **drops lemon essential oil**
- 2 **drops sweet orange essential oil**
- **lemon juice**

1. Place linseed oil, ¼ cup lemon juice, and waxes in a double boiler over low heat. Stir constantly until completely melted and smooth.
2. Add the essential oils. Remove from heat and pour the mixture into a clean coffee can and allow to harden.

3. Once the wax has hardened, tap the sides of the can until the wax breaks free. Turn out the wax and gently rub it on the floor, like a crayon. Saturate a cloth with lemon juice, wring out, and rub the wax tracings well into the floor. Buff with a clean, dry cloth.

Woodsy Wood Floor Wax

This formula leaves behind a nice shine and an earthy scent.

- **2 cups linseed oil**
- **¼ cup carnauba wax**
- **2 tablespoons beeswax**
- **¼ cup lemon juice**
- **8 drops patchouli essential oil**
- **10 drops cedar essential oil**
- **lemon juice**

1. Combine linseed oil, waxes, and the ¼ cup lemon juice in a double boiler over low heat. Stir constantly until all the wax is melted.
2. Add the essential oils and blend well. Remove from heat. Pour into a clean coffee can and allow to cool.
3. Once the wax has hardened, tap the sides of the can until the wax breaks free. Turn out the wax and gently rub it on the floor, like a crayon.
4. Saturate a cloth with lemon juice, wring out, and rub the wax tracings well into the floor. Buff with a clean, dry cloth.

Wax Remover

This formula is for wood floors without a protective varnish finish.

- 2 cups warm vinegar
- ½ cup lemon juice
- ½ cup water
- 1 capful liquid castile soap
- 10 drops essential oil of choice

Combine all ingredients. Dampen a sponge mop or soft-bristled brush with the formula and apply to the floor in sections, using short strokes. Wipe each floor section dry with a towel or clean mop before moving on to the next.

Solutions for Wood Problems

Black heel marks. These can be removed by rubbing 2 or 3 drops of cedar or eucalyptus essential oil over the mark with a soft cloth.

Burns. For burns that have not penetrated the wood surface but have just left a mark, rub with a thin paste of rottenstone (or cigarette ashes), linseed oil, and 2 or 3 drops of peppermint or tea tree essential oil. (*Note:* Tea tree oil is not recommended for dark wood.) If the burn has penetrated the wood surface, you may have to refinish the area.

Crayon. Wipe crayon marks with a few drops of cedar, peppermint, or tea tree essential oil mixed with a dab of toothpaste. (*Note:* Tea tree oil is not recommended for dark wood.) Wipe clean with a cloth moistened with vinegar.

Grease on floors. Immediately place ice cubes on top of the spill to harden and prevent the grease from seeping further into the wood. If a grease layer forms, it can be scraped off with a blunt object, such as a popsicle stick. If the wood is unfinished or has a penetrating finish, squirt some vegetable oil soap and a few drops of eucalyptus essential oil over the spill. Blot the stain repeatedly with clean paper towels or cotton cloths.

Painted wood floors. Wood floors that have been painted can be cleaned with a solution of 2 teaspoons washing soda and 1 cup rosemary or sage tea (strained and cooled) mixed with a gallon of warm water.

Scratches. For light-colored woods, wet a soft cloth with equal parts of lemon juice and olive or vegetable oil and gently rub into the wood. Scratches on walnut can be treated with — what else? — a freshly shelled raw walnut. Darker woods, like mahogany, can be treated with a cloth dipped in equal amounts of warm water and vinegar. If the scratch remains, you can fill it in with a crayon or oil pastel pencil. Scratch marks on wood floors may be removed by gently rubbing in a circular motion with very fine steel wool moistened with a hard wax, such as Citrus-Scented Wood Floor Wax (page 110) or Woodsy Wood Floor Wax (page 111).

Water stains and rings. Leaking vases and flowerpots or condensation from cold drink glasses can leave bleached rings on wood surfaces. To treat these stains, first remove old polish by wiping with a soft cloth dipped in full-strength vinegar. Wipe thoroughly with a dry cloth. Then apply mayonnaise or linseed oil, working from the outside to the center of the spot. Leave the oil or mayonnaise for several hours and then buff with a cloth. You can also rub 2 to 4 drops of peppermint essential oil on the stain. Toothpaste is reputedly another cure for water rings on wood. Whatever method you use, remember to test on an inconspicuous spot first.

CLEANING METALS

METAL POLISHES MAY CONTAIN ONE OR MORE strong acids that quickly dissolve tarnish. These acids can also burn human skin. Hydrofluoric acid, used in some rust removers and aluminum polishes, is probably the most hazardous. If it gets on your skin it continues to penetrate until it permeates the bone. Of course, protective gloves should be worn when handling such chemicals but, in spite of any precautions taken, does this sound like something you want to put your hands in? Worse yet, do you want to use it on utensils and vessels that are used to serve food?

Removing Metal Stains & Buildup

Many people are convinced that a caustic commercial polish is necessary to adequately perform the task of removing rust and tarnish from metals. But you probably already have the ingredients readily available in your kitchen or garden to do the job safely and to do it well. You may not have the instant results that might be achieved with a commercial polish, but you will get good results if you allow some time for the formulas suggested here to work. Besides, rust and tarnish do not develop overnight, why expect them to disappear in a moment?

Aluminum

Aluminum is the most abundant metal found in the earth's crust and is usually found as aluminum silicate or mixed with other minerals such as iron, calcium, and magnesium. Since the expense of extracting the aluminum from these silicate mixtures is too great, bauxite, an impure hydrated oxide, is the common source of commercial aluminum.

When in contact with air, new aluminum quickly forms a durable oxide layer that protects it from corrosion. This layer is why aluminum products never rust or tarnish. Aluminum is, however, highly reactive, and two commonly used ingredients in homemade metal cleaners should never be used on it: baking soda and washing soda.

Since aluminum resists corrosion and tarnish, superficial stains are the only problems to contend with. Spruce up your aluminum by cleaning with one of these methods:

Vinegar–Citrus Solution. In a sink or a plastic tub, mix 2 cups of boiled water, 1 cup of vinegar, and 1 teaspoon of any citrus essential oil. Place items in the solution and let soak for an hour or more. Rinse and dry well before storing.

Cornstarch–Citrus Paste. Combine 2 tablespoons cornstarch, 2 tablespoons alum, 5 drops of lemon or orange essential oil, and enough water to make a thick paste. While wearing gloves, rub onto metal until clean. Rinse and dry well.

Cream of Tartar–Citrus Paste. Make a paste of ¼ cup vinegar and 2 tablespoons cream of tartar; add 2 to 4 drops of a citrus essential oil, if desired. Spread the paste on the metal and rub with your glove-protected fingers until it is clean. Rinse and dry well.

Rhubarb (or Tomato) Soak. For utensils, place 1 cup of sliced rhubarb in 2 cups of water (or enough water to submerge the items in a pot. Simmer for 30 minutes. Rinse utensils in cool water and dry. *Note:* Fresh or canned tomato slices can be used in place of the rhubarb.

Brass

Brass is an alloy of copper and zinc. Most brass items acquired in recent years will have a lacquer finish to retard tarnish. You can maintain the shine of these items with a weekly dusting and an occasional bath in warm, sudsy water. Never use hot water to clean brass items or the lacquer finish may begin to peel away from the metal. After cleaning, you can polish the brass to a shine with a bit of olive oil, which will help to resist tarnish.

Older pieces of brass will oxidize over time and become tarnished, developing a greenish tinge. Here are a few ways to restore brass to its original beauty:

Citrus Salt Paste. Dissolve 4 drops of any citrus essential oil and 2 teaspoons of salt in 1 cup of vinegar. Add just enough all-purpose flour to make a thick paste. Smear the paste onto the brass and rub with a dry sponge. Let the paste completely dry, then rinse in warm water. Dry and polish to a shine.

Citrus Vinegar Paste. Combine ¼ cup vinegar, ¼ cup Worcestershire sauce, 3 drops lemon essential oil, and 3 drops grapefruit seed extract. Using a soft sponge, apply this solution to the metal and rub well. If the item is very tarnished, let it soak for 30 minutes or more in this solution. Then rinse and dry thoroughly.

Milk Bath. Soak your brass pieces in 1 cup of warm water and 1 cup of milk (or more for larger pieces — just use equal parts of milk and water). Milk contains lactic acid, a natural solvent.

Lemon—Cream of Tartar Paste. Make a paste of ¼ cup lemon juice, 4 to 6 drops of orange or lemon essential oil, and 2 to 3 tablespoons cream of tartar. Rub the paste on with your fingers (wear protective gloves) using small circular motions. Let the paste dry. Then rinse and dry with a cloth.

SPECIAL CASES

You need to be careful when cleaning antique brass items so that you don't disturb the aged coloring of the piece, or what is referred to as its patina.

The best way to clean most pieces is to start with a bath in warm soapy water to remove filmy dirt and grease. Then polish with a soft cloth moistened in linseed oil. Brass andirons should be cleaned with extrafine steel wool, rubbing the metal in one direction only.

If you have a very old or delicate piece and are not sure how to approach cleaning it, you may want to consult with an expert, such as an antiques dealer, refinisher, or museum curator.

Bronze

Bronze is also an alloy of copper, but unlike brass, it is combined with almost any other metal but zinc. Like brass, however, solid bronze pieces are often lacquered to prevent tarnishing. Good quality bronze pieces, especially those displayed outdoors, develop a lovely patina as they age. Since this weathered effect is highly desirable in bronze, regular dusting and light polishing with a soft cloth are generally all you need to do. A soft brush can be used on items that have been neglected for a time. If you want a high polish on a bronze item, wipe it clean and then shine it with a cloth dipped in a liquid wax.

Bronze is also susceptible to bronze disease, characterized by isolated spots of corrosion and light green patches. This spotting is caused by exposure to chlorides, sulfides, or excessive moisture. Usually, this disease can be remedied by bathing the piece in boiled distilled water, changing the water several times during the process. It may be necessary to soak the item for several days. You can also use hot vinegar and salt, or even hot buttermilk. If these treatments don't cure the problem, you'll need to call an expert.

To clean dirt and grease from bronze, pull on protective gloves and rub the item vigorously with a cloth moistened with a solution of 1 cup vinegar, $\frac{1}{8}$ cup grapefruit juice, and 6 drops pine or cedar essential oil. Rinse in warm water and dry completely with a soft, clean towel.

Cast Iron

My father is a native of Alabama, where cornbread is a staple and often made in a cast-iron skillet. My family had such a skillet, and one day, I decided to give the pan a good scrubbing with soap and water and left it to air-dry in the dish rack. When I returned to put the pan away I puzzled over how it became dirty looking again. In fact, it looked worse than before! My mistake, of course, was in letting the pan air-dry and form rust.

Cast iron will oxidize and rust if not kept completely dry at all times. It must also be seasoned with oil to form a protective barrier and prevent oxidation. When you acquire a new piece of cast iron, you need to clean it with a mild soap and fine steel wool and dry it by hand immediately. Then the interior should be wiped with a bit of vegetable oil and the pan set in a low oven (250°F) for two hours. After the pan has cooled, wipe it out and wash once more, taking care to dry it thoroughly. Now the pan is properly seasoned and ready to use.

After each use, cast iron should be wiped and quickly washed and dried. Another application of oil is needed before storing the pan. Cast iron pans should not be stored with the lids in place, as this can trap moisture. It's also a good idea to place a paper towel inside the pan when storing to absorb excess moisture. If it becomes necessary to scour cast iron to remove cooked-on foods, it will be necessary to reseason the pan.

Chrome

Chrome is a hard metal with a whitish-blue appearance. Its durability and shine make it suitable for plating other metals to extend the life of the object. Chrome, or chromium, is frequently found on appliances such as toasters, ovens, refrigerators, faucets, vehicles — even golf clubs. If kept free of grease and sticky grime, chrome can last a very long time. *Note*: Never use an abrasive cleaner on chrome that may scratch or pit the surface.

To safely clean chrome, apply club soda or vinegar with a soft cloth. Dry to a shine with a dry cloth.

To remove burned-on grease, clean with 3 to 6 drops of undiluted eucalyptus or peppermint essential oil (wear protective gloves). Wipe dry with a clean cloth.

For rust stains, first clean with a rag and a few drops of eucalyptus or peppermint essential oil. Then rub the stains with a small piece of crumpled aluminum foil, shiny side out. Wipe well with a soft cloth moistened with 3 to 6 drops of essential oil and 1 tablespoon of jojoba or almond oil (mix them first).

Copper

Decorative copper items are usually coated with lacquer to preserve the finish; they should never be polished. Only regular dusting and periodic washing are necessary. Copper cookware and utensils, on the other hand, may need special handling to remove any factory-applied lacquer. Follow the manufacturer's directions; if there aren't any instructions included, the copper pieces should be placed in 2 gallons of boiling water and 1½ cups washing soda. Let them soak until you are able to peel away the lacquer.

Stainless steel pots and pans often have copper bottoms for better distribution of heat, but high temperatures can damage them. Never scour copper bottoms with steel wool or an abrasive cleanser. If tarnishing occurs, use equal amounts of salt, flour, and vinegar to make a polishing paste.

To clean and remove tarnish from copper pots and utensils, try one of these tricks:

Citrus–Salt Rub. Cut a lime or lemon in half, sprinkle with salt, and rub over the copper. If you don't have any fresh lemons or limes on hand, you can use lemon juice or 1 teaspoon of any citrus essential oil mixed with 2 tablespoons water instead. Apply this solution to a damp sponge that has been sprinkled with salt. Nothing can be easier than this!

Citrus-Vinegar Paste. Make a paste of 1 cup vinegar, 5 drops citrus essential oil, 1¼ cups all-purpose flour, and ½ cup salt. Spread the paste on your copper pieces and let stand for a few hours, or overnight. Then rinse, dry, and polish with a bit of oil to prevent further tarnishing.

Ketchup Blend. Mix ½ cup ketchup with 2 tablespoons cream of tartar. Spread on the copper and let stand for an hour. Rinse in soapy water and then in clean water. Dry thoroughly.

COPPER CAUTIONS

Copper can also be vulnerable to bronze disease. Follow the suggestions given on page 120 to tackle this problem.

Pots or bowls with copper interiors cannot be used for preparing or storing acidic foods such as fruits, tomatoes, or anything containing vinegar. These foods can react with copper to form toxic compounds.

Pewter

Antique pewter is an alloy of lead and tin. Old pewter develops a dark patina over time that looks beautiful, but due to the lead content, such pieces cannot be used to prepare or serve foods. Most pewter pieces made today are tarnish resistant, being composed of roughly 90 percent tin and 10 percent copper or antimony. This combination of metals retains its original color and is lead-free, but is not as durable and is vulnerable to dents and scratches. Some imitation pewter pieces are made from aluminum. To be safe, check the manufacturer's instructions for the appropriate care and cleaning of individual items. Try these quick fixes for your pewter pieces:

Cabbage. Pewter can be cleaned by rubbing with wet cabbage leaves or freshly cut leaf wedges.

Minty Paste. Revive dull pewter with a paste made from ¼ cup fine rottenstone, 2 teaspoons linseed oil, and 4 drops peppermint or wintergreen essential oil. (Go easy — it's supposed to have a dark color due to its lead content.)

Salt Paste. You can also clean pewter pieces with a solution of 1 teaspoon salt dissolved in 1 cup vinegar. Add 4 drops essential oil of choice and enough all-purpose flour to make a paste. Rub onto the metal with glove-protected fingertips. Rinse well and dry thoroughly.

Silver

Silver has many seemingly innocent enemies. Rubber, for instance, not only promotes tarnishing when in contact with silver, it can actually corrode the finish. Using rubber gloves while cleaning silver is definitely not a good idea. Likewise, avoid storing silver in rubber-lined cabinets or storage boxes. Even binding silver pieces together with rubber bands can prove detrimental.

Other substances that have a negative impact on silver include olives, eggs, salad dressing, fruit juices, vinegar, and salt. And, believe it or not, flowers should never be placed in a silver vase unless it is lined with a glass or plastic container first. As cut flowers decompose they release an acid that can permanently etch silver finishes.

Sterling silver is actually an alloy of approximately 92.5 percent silver and 7.5 percent copper; plated silver has a layer of silver electroplated over another metal. All silver readily oxidizes and responds to hand polishing for the best sheen and patina. The best course of action to deter tarnishing of silver flatware is to use it often, but never allow food to stand. If you can't wash it right away, rinse off any food residue until you can give your flatware a proper cleaning. (*Note:* Some decorative pieces may be lacquered; care should be taken to avoid contact with hot water.) When silver is not in use, it should be stored rolled up in a flannel cloth.

If you put your silver flatware in the dishwasher, it's best to hand-dry the items instead of letting them go through the heated drying cycle. Also, it's important to separate silver flatware from other pieces, such as stainless steel, in the silverware basket of your dishwasher to avoid scratching or possible chemical reactions with other materials.

If you have a problem with tarnish, here are a couple of formulas to try:

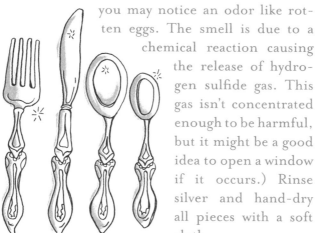

Easy Tarnish Remover. Place silver pieces in a sink or pan filled with water. Add 2 tablespoons cream of tartar and a few strips of aluminum foil. Let the silver soak for an hour or until tarnish free. (If the silver is badly tarnished, you may notice an odor like rotten eggs. The smell is due to a chemical reaction causing the release of hydrogen sulfide gas. This gas isn't concentrated enough to be harmful, but it might be a good idea to open a window if it occurs.) Rinse silver and hand-dry all pieces with a soft cloth.

Instant Tarnish Remover. Squeeze some ordinary toothpaste into a small bowl and add 3 to 5 drops of peppermint or spearmint essential oil. Rub this mixture with your fingertips onto the silver. As the tarnish is removed, the toothpaste mixture will turn grayish. Rinse the silver well and hand-dry thoroughly before storing. Since gloves shouldn't be worn while cleaning silver, wash hands well when finished. If your skin begins to itch while using the cleaner, rinse well.

WHAT ABOUT GOLD?

Gold is soft metal and can easily be scratched by abrasives. The safest way to clean gold is with a paste of 1 teaspoon liquid castile soap and 1 tablespoon baking soda. Using your fingertips, gently rub the paste onto the item. Rinse in warm water and dry thoroughly with a soft cloth or towel.

CHAPTER 7

WALLS & CARPETING

DIRT AND GERMS ARE EVERYWHERE, under our feet and surrounding us on all sides. Hopefully, we don't think too much about this fact of life, or we'd start to feel a bit antsy about sitting on the floor. While cohabiting with a few germs in our life is beneficial to our health, it's probably wise to draw the line at allowing an entire ecosystem from gaining a foothold in the carpeting. And who likes to look at dreary, stained walls?

Wallpaper and carpeting are really semipermanent fixtures. You can replace your living room drapes in a flash if you've grown tired of looking at them. But can you say the same about your bathroom wallpaper or den carpeting? The cost of these accessories isn't a casual matter either. It makes good sense, then, to use safe, organic products to care for your investment. Not only are they better for you and the environment, but they will help to preserve the color and texture of wall coverings and carpet fibers.

Keeping Walls Clean

With three boys in our house, fingerprints on walls are just a part of life. The frequency of prints has lessened to a great extent in recent years, but when the boys were younger, the perpetual mural of hand- and fingerprints along the stairway could almost represent a daily growth chart. Of course, the kids loved earning a little money by taking on extra chores each Saturday, and cleaning off those fingerprints was one of the first tasks offered.

Walls painted with semigloss paint are the easiest to clean since they have a slick coating that doesn't absorb liquids. In fact, this type of paint is preferred for kitchens, and especially for children's rooms, where a lot can happen to a wall. Latex can also be washed, but lightly. Scrubbing and repeated application of moisture may remove not only dirt and stains but the paint as well. The best way to clean painted walls is to use a solution of equal parts of vinegar and water. To a full spray bottle of solution add 6 to 10 drops of your favorite essential oil for grease-cutting power. Just make sure to use a clear or light essential oil on walls, such as eucalyptus, mint, or tea tree. (*Note:* Tea tree oil should be used on white walls only.)

Most wallpaper made today is washable, with some even being labeled as "scrubbable." Washable papers usually have a thin plastic film; scrubbable papers are either coated or impregnated with vinyl. In truth, you really can't scrub either one, nor should you use abrasive cleansers that could mar the paper's protective coating. The right way to clean wallpaper is to use small circular motions with a soapy cloth or sponge. The paper should then be wiped with a damp sponge and dried with a clean towel or cloth. If it becomes necessary to wash an area a second time, the paper must be allowed to dry thoroughly first. Over-wetting wallpaper can cause the glue on the backing to dissolve, and soon your beautiful paper will be on the floor, not on your wall.

Wallpapered walls should be dusted frequently to reduce the risk of staining and streaking, and is especially necessary in the kitchen and bathroom, where hot water and steam can encourage a film to develop on dirty wallpaper. If you have a wall brush attachment with your vacuum cleaner, you can use it to dust your walls. If not, an old broom or mop handle with clean rags attached to one end will suffice.

Safe & Simple Wall Formulas

The following formulas will enable you to safely clean painted walls and wallpaper. If you have a stain removal issue and know that you have nonwashable wallpaper, consult the manufacturer or check with the store where it was purchased for cleaning recommendations. Regardless of what type of paper or paint covers your walls, always test a cleaning formula on a small area for a reaction before attempting to clean the entire surface.

All-Purpose Citrus Wall Cleaner

This general formula is a good one to safely clean wall surfaces.

- 1 cup water
- ½ cup vinegar
- 6 drops lemon, grapefruit, or orange essential oil

Combine all ingredients in a plastic spray bottle. Shake vigorously before each use. Lightly spray the affected areas of your wall and wipe with a clean, damp sponge. If you're working on a stain and it's still visible after the area has completely air-dried, see the tips for cleaning walls on pages 134–136.

Disinfectant Thyme Formula

This recipe is great for cleaning wall surfaces in a child's room, as well as light switches, the sides of the crib, or wherever little fingers tend to leave smudges and germs.

- **1 cup water**
- **1 cup vinegar**
- **5 drops tea tree essential oil**
- **3 drops thyme essential oil**

Combine all ingredients in a plastic spray bottle. Lightly spray the affected areas of your wall and wipe with a clean, damp sponge. Give a final wipe to surfaces with a sponge or cloth moistened with plain water.

THE FLOOR-TO-CEILING SOLUTION

Always clean walls by working from the bottom up to the ceiling. This advice may seem odd to you, but there is good reason for it. If you've ever tried the reverse — cleaning from top to bottom — then you've probably experienced those drip lines that travel down the wall and stay there. Those streaks of cleaning product have been working ahead of you and are very difficult to get rid of. This problem is eliminated if you take the floor-to-ceiling approach.

Minty Wall Cleansing Paste

This cleanser is nonabrasive and will dissolve grease and finger-prints. It is recommended for use on washable papers or semigloss painted walls that are usually found in the kitchen, bathroom, and children's bedrooms. **Note:** *The small amount of tea tree oil will not harm colored wallpaper.*

¼ cup concentrated oil soap paste (available in health food and hardware stores)

2 drops peppermint essential oil

2 drops spearmint essential oil

2 drops tea tree essential oil

Put the soap paste in a short, widemouthed glass jar, such as a clean baby food jar. Add the essential oils and blend well. It will have the consistency of jelly. Dip a damp cloth into the soap paste and squish the cloth between your fingers to make suds. Apply to wallpaper; rinse with another clean, damp cloth or sponge. Follow up with a dry cloth or towel.

Helpful Hints for Cleaning Walls

Stains and spots on nonwashable papers may be dealt with by rubbing a pencil eraser or art gum over them. The same applies to pencil marks. Or rub a freshly cut rhubarb stalk over the stain and wipe with a damp cloth. Test both methods on a small area out of view first.

Got a grease stain? Tear or cut a paper towel into four squares. To one square apply 1 or 2 drops of eucalyptus essential oil and allow it to dry. Using an iron on a low setting, press the oil-treated paper towel square against the grease stain for a few seconds. Then immediately press a clean paper towel square against the stain. Repeat this procedure with the remaining paper towel squares. If the grease stain remains, wait a few hours and apply a thick paste of cream of tartar, baking soda, and enough water to hold everything together. Brush the paste away when it has dried to a powder. If both of these methods fail, consider repainting or start shopping for new wallpaper.

Crayon scribbling on painted walls or wallpaper can be tough to tackle. Fortunately, most crayons are washable today, but the nonwashable type are still around. Try the methods described above for removing grease spots. If the crayon mark endures, and if it's on a painted surface, scrub (yes, scrub) the area with liquid castile soap and 1 or 2 drops of orange essential oil. I wouldn't try this on wallpaper (unless you think yours might hold up), but you should be able to remove it from a painted wall without causing too much damage. A weathered look on the wall is better than waxy lines of color.

Food stains, especially spaghetti sauce, always seem to make impossible leaps from the simmering pot on the stove to the kitchen wall several feet away (and onto everything in between). If wiped right away there's usually no problem. But we never seem to notice these stains until we go looking for them, usually before a party or important entertaining event. If the wall is covered with washable paint or wallpaper, your task is less daunting; just wipe it with the All-Purpose Citrus Wall Cleaner (see page 132). If the wall is covered with latex paint or nonwashable wallpaper, you may have more trouble. Carefully scrape off as much as you can with a blunt object or dull knife. If a noticeable stain remains, place 3 drops of eucalyptus essential oil on a cotton ball and then dip it in baking soda. Dab the stain with the cotton ball a few times and then rub until the stain disappears.

Deep Cleaning the Carpets?

To a lot of people, the term "deep cleaning" seems to conjure up a vision of a sea of foaming suds and water whisking away dirt from "way under." All that soapy sloshing must really get a carpet clean, right?

Wrong. Too much soap and water will leave a residue in the carpet that acts like a magnet for dirt. And getting the backing of the carpet wet only creates a pool for the dirt (and stains) to collect in, not to mention promoting the potential for mildew and shrinkage of the carpet. So the first rule of carpet cleaning in terms of cleaning products is "less is more."

If you've ever steamed or shampooed your carpet by machine and have had to empty the collection tank, then you're already aware of how much gunk lives in the carpet fibers. In addition to minute pieces of sand and dead skin, there's a host of nasty critters such as mites and, if you have pets, fleas. All of these will ruin carpet fibers if given free reign. Frequent vacuuming (at least once each week) will displace these critters and their food source at the same time. Heavy traffic areas, such as hallways, stairs, and foyers, can be swept with a broom or a carpet sweeper before vacuuming. This helps to lift the nap of the carpet and bring soil to the surface for easier removal.

Do-It-Yourself Carpet Remedies

Just like the little fingerprints on our walls, foot-prints and spills of uncertain origin are not strangers to our wall-to-wall carpeting. Exercise the familiar "please, wipe your feet" as often as you will, but energy-driven kids in muddy sneakers often forget to pause at the doormat. This section offers some safe herbal and alternative solutions for cleaning carpets, as well as tips for treating some pretty sticky messes.

Simple Rug & Carpet Deodorizer

Pets and bare feet can cause a rather funky smell. This formula leaves your carpets looking and smelling fresh again.

> 1   cup borax
> 1   cup baking soda
> ½   cup cornmeal
> 10 drops juniper essential oil
> 5   drops cypress essential oil

Combine the dry ingredients in a plastic bowl. Add essential oils and mix well, breaking up clumps. Sprinkle the mixture over carpet and wait several hours, overnight if possible, before vacuuming.

Peppermint Foam Carpet Shampoo

This formula is great for cleaning heavy traffic areas.

- 3   cups water
- ¾   cup vegetable-based liquid soap
- 10 drops peppermint essential oil

Mix all ingredients in a blender. Rub the foam into soiled areas with a damp sponge. Let dry thoroughly and then vacuum.

Herbal Rug Restorer

Alum and vinegar combine to clean and lift carpet fibers. The essential oils leave a fresh herbal scent. Note: *For spot treatment, rub a little baking soda into soiled areas. Let dry and brush clean with a soft–bristled brush; follow with Rug Restorer. Use gloves if your hands will be coming in contact with the cleaner.*

- ½   gallon hot water
- ½   cup alum
- ¼   cup vinegar
- 8   drops rosemary essential oil
- 3   drops lemon essential oil

Combine all ingredients in a pail or bucket. Fill a second bucket with hot water for rinsing. Dip a clean sponge mop into the vinegar solution, squeeze out excess liquid, and wipe over carpet in sections. Rinse the mop in the second bucket between cleaning sections and squeeze out excess water. Repeat until all of the carpet has been cleaned.

Rosemary-Lavender Carpet Shampoo

This recipe makes enough for a 10 × 13' room. If you can't find soap flakes, you may use ¼ cup of borax instead, but test the outcome of this substitution on a small area first.

2   cups baking soda
½   cup soap flakes
20 drops lavender essential oil
8   drops rosemary essential oil
½   cup vinegar
2   cups warm water

1. Sweep the carpet to be cleaned with a broom or carpet sweeper to loosen dirt, then vacuum the entire area. Combine the baking soda and soap flakes in a plastic bowl. Add the essential oils and mix well, breaking up any clumps with a fork. Sprinkle the mixture on the carpet.

2. Add the vinegar to the warm water in a bucket or pail. Dip a clean sponge mop into the bucket and squeeze out as much excess liquid as you can. Gently go over the carpet with the sponge mop, working in sections. Wait at least an hour and then vacuum again.

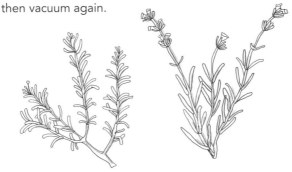

Fleas-Be-Gone Carpet Treatment

Try this excellent formula to rid yourself of those pesky little critters. It may seem wasteful, but it's best to get rid of the vacuum cleaner bag after this treatment to prevent reinfestation of fleas.

- 2½ cups baking soda
- 10 drops sweet orange essential oil
- 10 drops citronella essential oil
- 8 drops peppermint or spearmint essential oil
- 6 drops lemon or lemon balm essential oil

Vacuum carpet well. Combine all ingredients in a plastic container and sprinkle on carpet. Wait at least one hour before vacuuming again.

Natural Carpet Steamer Solutions

I've received many requests for natural formulas for steam carpet cleaners since the first edition of this book came out. The wait is over!

The proportions given in these formulas are intended for one-time use. Reduce or increase the volume of formula according to the type of machine you have and the amount of cleaning solution it can hold. You can also make any of these formulas in larger amounts and store for later use. Always test for colorfastness on an inconspicuous area of carpet before using a formula for the first time.

Thyme to Make Your Own Carpet Steamer Shampoo

The thyme in this formula offers antibacterial properties and a very refreshing scent. In fact, this herb received its name from the Greek word **thymon** *which translates to mean "to fumigate."*

- ¾ cup very hot water
- ½ cup white vinegar
- 1 tablespoon liquid castile soap
- 30 drops thyme essential oil

Pour all ingredients into a container with a pour spout (or use a funnel to dispense) and blend well. Add the formula to the appropriate compartment of your steam cleaner. Clean your carpet according to the manufacturer's instructions.

A LIGHT HAND

Be careful not to saturate a carpet when using liquid cleaners, or even water. If the backing gets wet, the invading stain will have a safe place to hide and it will be much more difficult to remove.

Heavy Duty Herbal Carpet Steamer Formula

This formula packs a punch when it comes to cutting grease and cleaning tough dirt from carpeting.

- ¾ cup very hot water
- ½ cup white vinegar
- 1 tablespoon hydrogen peroxide (omit for dark-colored carpet)
- 1 tablespoon liquid castile soap
- 1 tablespoon powdered citric acid
- 20 drops grapefruit seed extract

Combine all ingredients into a container or bowl. Blend well to evenly distribute the ingredients. Pour the formula into your steam cleaner and proceed to clean your carpet.

Helpful Hints for Cleaning Carpeting

Spills should be cleaned up as soon as possible. Always blot a stain with towels or cloths to absorb excess liquid. Rubbing the stain vigorously can cause further penetration of the spill into the carpet fibers and backing.

Most food stains can be safely removed with a solution of vinegar and a bit of dishwashing soap. You can add a few drops of essential oil to the vinegar first if you like.

Blood stains and spots should be blotted with cold water or club soda. If the stain doesn't come out completely, use a cloth moistened with cold water and 2 drops eucalyptus essential oil.

Sprinkle mud stains with salt or baking soda. Wait 30 minutes, then vacuum.

For ink stains, first cover with cream of tartar. Then take a fresh lemon wedge and squeeze a few drops of juice over the cream of tartar. Using the flesh of the lemon, gently go over the spot a few times. Brush away the powder and blot with a damp sponge.

Urine stains should first be blotted with paper towels to absorb as much of the liquid as possible. With a sponge, apply a solution of ¼ cup vinegar, 1 teaspoon dishwashing soap, and 8 to 10 drops of peppermint or eucalyptus essential oil; wait 20 minutes. (The vinegar and essential oils will help to sanitize the soiled area and remove any odor.) Blot the stained area again using a clean, damp towel. *Note:* Vinegar can sometimes slightly bleach dark-colored carpets. Test this formula on an inconspicuous area first.

CHAPTER

8

CLEARING THE AIR

IN MEDIEVAL EUROPE, herbs and spices played an important role in the maintenance of the household, not only for their culinary qualities, but also for their ability to mask unpleasant odors caused by poor hygiene and unsanitary conditions.

Today, although we may no longer be plagued by insufficient sanitation, we have a new challenge to face from modern household materials: Ordinary carpeting, furniture, and painted surfaces all produce toxic vapors such as VOCs (volatile organic compounds), trichlorethylene, and formaldehyde. Obviously, unless we choose to live in a tent, we cannot escape or avoid every contaminant found in building materials. But we can greatly reduce their impact on our health by purifying the air to minimize their presence in the home. How? By developing a green thumb.

Clean & Green

You may recall from high school biology that plants are involved in a process called photosynthesis. During this process, plants continuously take in carbon dioxide and other airborne toxins to produce oxygen. Bingo! You've got instant air filtration. In fact, it has been estimated that 15 to 20 spider plants will effectively detoxify a home of less than 2,000 square feet. Of course, almost any type of plant will help to do the same.

If you're wondering where you are going to put all these plants, consider hanging baskets, plant stands that can hold several plants at a time, or even mini gardens on windowsills. If natural lighting is a problem, artificial lighting, such as grow lights, will keep your living air purifiers healthy. If you have little ones or pets, be sure to keep plants — especially poisonous ones — out of their reach.

Some common plants that purify air are:

* Spider plant, also known as airplane plant (*Chlorophytum comosum* 'vittatum')
* Golden pothos (*Epipremnum* aureum)
* Peace lily (*Spathiphyllum* species)
* Fern (*Pteris* species and *Nephrolepsis* species)
* Chinese evergreen (*Aglaonema modestum* 'Silver Queen')
* Weeping fig (*Ficus benjamina*)

Herbs also filter the air, and many can easily be grown indoors year-round. Basil, thyme, oregano, sage, rosemary, mints, and geraniums are just some herbs that not only help to clean the air but offer aromatic properties of their own, not to mention adding flavor to your favorite dishes.

Potpourri

Potpourri gets its name from a marriage of the French words *pot* (which means the same in English) and *pourri* (which means "to rot") — collectively, "rotting pot." One modern definition of potpourri is a literary or musical medley; for our purposes, it's a harmonic composition of botanical fragrances.

There is essentially no end to the different types of potpourri that you can create. All successful dried formulas require a fixative, which captures the aromatic oils from flowers, spices, and herbs when blended together. Common fixatives include orrisroot (the dried, ground rhizome of the iris plant), oakmoss, calamus root (sweet flag), gum benzoin, frankincense, cinnamon sticks, and patchouli. Fixatives can also take the form of woody material, such as pinecones, milkweed pods, and cedar shavings or chips. Some craft stores carry a fixative made from dried corncobs.

The base of a potpourri is made of dried aromatic herbs and plants, and may include flowers, stems, and leaves. Spices such as cloves, ginger, and nutmeg are also used in making potpourri blends. Fragrant herbal essential oils add concentrated aroma to potpourri and are easily obtainable. Pieces of dried bark, berries, fruit peels, and unusual seedpods are not only attractive, but also act as fixatives and help to preserve the scent. Bear in mind, however, that trial and error is often necessary to achieve the right balance in a potpourri, especially in its application. For instance, some potpourri ingredients may smell strong in the dry form, but are lost to other ingredients that prevail when simmered in water.

It isn't necessary to add a fixative to a potpourri intended to be simmered unless you desire additional fragrance. Do not add benzoin to a simmering potpourri; although it has a nice fragrance in dried form, it is rather unpleasant when simmered. The key to making interesting potpourri blends lies in your desire to experiment, but many variations are offered here to spark your imagination.

Blending Your Own Potpourri

Making potpourri is easy. It takes moments to mix, then requires only a few seconds for a daily shake. As the weeks go on, you'll notice the scent changing, becoming mellower.

* * *

These simple steps apply to the 15 blends that follow.

1. Combine all ingredients in a wide-mouthed glass jar and stir with a spoon until well blended.
2. Cap the jar and leave it in a place free of drafts, direct sunlight, and extreme temperatures.
3. Gently shake the jar once a day for 4 to 6 weeks, or until you feel that the fragrance has fully developed.

A Midsummer's Eve

This outdoorsy potpourri may be added to pillows and sachets or set out in a dish or bowl.

- ½ cup *each* purple basil, chamomile, and marjoram
- ¼ cup *each* yarrow (white or yellow), juniper berries, and oakmoss
- 2 tablespoons *each* gum benzoin and mace
- 1 teaspoon grated orange peel
- 15 drops cedar essential oil

Sinful Seduction

Add this potpourri to pillows and sachets or set out in a dish or bowl. Note: *Tonka beans, members of the pea family, are flavorless yet contain a strong vanilla–like scent. You can find them in health food stores.*

- 1 cup *each* jasmine flowers and lemon verbena leaves
- ½ cup *each* chopped gingerroot and crushed clary sage leaves
- 2 tonka beans
- 1 vanilla bean, chopped into small pieces
- 1 tablespoon *each* sandalwood chips and cumin seed
- 20 drops patchouli essential oil

NOTE: *See page 149 for basic potpourri blending instructions.*

Elegant Romance

A lovely potpourri, Elegant Romance may be simmered in a pan of hot water on the stove, added to pillows and sachets, or set out in a dish or bowl.

- 1 cup *each* rose petals, lavender buds, and geranium leaves
- ½ cup *each* lemon verbena leaves and powdered orrisroot
- 10 drops vanilla fragrance oil
- 8 drops sandalwood essential oil

SAVING SANDALWOOD

Sandalwood is highly valued in the perfume industry for its rich scent. The oil is extracted from the roots of a tree that can take up to 75 years to reach maturity. It doesn't grow in many places in the world, and given the current level of demand, the tree has the potential to become endangered. Always use sandalwood sparingly.

Spring Fresh

This strongly fragrant potpourri may be simmered in a pan of hot water on the stove, added to pillows and sachets, or set out in a dish or bowl.

- ½ cup *each* rosemary leaves, peppermint or spearmint leaves, and torn eucalyptus leaves
- ¼ cup *each* thyme leaves and whole cloves
- 2 teaspoons grated lemon peel
- 1 teaspoon grated orange peel

Country Roads

Simmer this autumn-scented potpourri in a pan of hot water on the stove, add it to pillows and sachets, or set it out in a pretty dish or bowl.

- 2 cups dried apple slices
- 1 cup *each* bay leaves and sage
- ½ cup *each* chopped, unpeeled gingerroot and whole cloves
- Eight 1-inch cinnamon sticks

Exotic Blend

Don't simmer this blend; instead, add it to pillows and sachets or set out in an unusual dish or bowl.

- ½ cup jasmine flowers
- ¼ cup *each* lemon verbena, lavender, sweet woodruff, and fennel leaves
- 2 teaspoons each coriander peel and gingerroot

Sweet Dreams

You can make this blend in larger quantities and sew it into herbal sleep pillows for a soothing effect. Stuff pillows and sachets with it, or set it out in a dish or bowl. You may use ¼ cup dill seed in place of the plant material.

½ cup *each* chamomile flowers; sweet clover flowers; dill stems, leaves, and flowers; lavender flowers; and sweet marjoram

¼ cup lemongrass or lemon balm leaves

FRUIT 'N SPICE

Make old-fashioned pomanders for your closets, your cabinets, or just about anywhere. Plenty of recipes abound on the internet, using any citrus fruit and a variety of spices, but the simplest version of all is to push whole cloves into the skin of an orange until it is completely covered. If needed, thread a string or ribbon through the middle and hang. The humble pomander's benefits are many: it freshens the air, the scents remind people of the holiday season, and the smell of orange and clove drives away several common pests.

NOTE: See page 149 for basic potpourri blending instructions.

Orange Delight

This spicy potpourri may be simmered in a pan of hot water on the stove, added to pillows and sachets, or set out in a dish or bowl.

2 cups orange peel, cut into small strips

1 cup *each* marigold flower heads and cubed dried apple

½ cup *each* whole cloves, cinnamon chips, and calamus root

10 drops sweet orange essential oil

Mulberry Madness

Displaying this potpourri in a bowl or dish will catch the attention of guests. You can also add the blend to pillows or sachets.

3 cups rose petals and leaves

1 cup *each* juniper berries and hibiscus flowers

½ cup crushed bay leaves

¼ cup star anise

2 tablespoons orrisroot

15 drops mulberry fragrance (liquid; available in craft stores)

NOTE: *See page 149 for basic potpourri blending instructions.*

Enchanted Hummingbird

This potpourri contains some noted hummingbird flowers. It may be added to pillows and sachets or set out in a dish or bowl.

- 1 cup *each* magnolia flowers, rose hips, bee balm blossoms, and lemon verbena
- ½ cup calendula flowers
- ¼ cup *each* grated orange peel and grated tangerine peel
- 2 tablespoons orrisroot
- 10 drops *each* rose geranium and bergamot essential oils

Woodland Breezes

You can use this potpourri to stuff pillows and sachets, or display it in an attractive dish or bowl.

- 1 cup *each* whole sage leaves, red nasturtium blossoms, evening primrose flowers, and cedar chips
- ½ cup *each* clary sage leaves and oakmoss
- ¼ cup angelica root, chopped
- 25 drops patchouli essential oil

Morning Dew

A light, fresh blend, this potpourri may be added to pillows and sachets or set out in a dish or bowl.

- 1 cup *each* lemon balm leaves and flowers, marigold blossoms, and peppermint leaves
- ½ cup *each* chamomile flowers and lemon thyme leaves
- ¼ cup *each* grated grapefruit peel and grated lemon peel
- 2 tablespoons coriander
- 1 tablespoon orrisroot
- 15 drops bergamot essential oil

Nice 'n Spicy

Nice 'n Spicy is a great simmering blend, but it also can be added to pillows and sachets or displayed in a dish or bowl.

- 1 cup *each* anise hyssop and fennel leaves
- ½ cup pineapple-scented sage
- ¼ cup grated orange peel
- 2 tablespoons aniseed, ground
- 1 tablespoon *each* coriander and caraway seeds
- 10 drops sandalwood essential oil
- 5 drops vanilla essential oil

NOTE: *See page 149 for basic potpourri blending instructions.*

Garden Memories

This colorful blend may be added to pillows and sachets or set out in a dish or bowl.

- 1 cup *each* calendula flowers, statice, cornflowers, and snapdragons
- ½ cup *each* rose petals, sunflower petals, marigolds, rose hips, and juniper berries
- ¼ cup *each* cedar chips and anise, ground
- 2 cinnamon sticks, crushed

Winter Blues Chaser

Have this potpourri on hand for the winter holidays. I save plenty of needles from our Christmas tree and wreath each year, so I always have a supply of balsam, cedar, or pine available. The potpourri may be simmered in a pan of hot water on the stove, added to pillows and sachets, or set out in a dish or bowl.

- 1 cup evergreen needles
- ½ cup *each* chopped dried apple, cedar chips, and cinnamon sticks, broken into small pieces
- ¼ cup whole cloves
- 1 tablespoon *each* allspice berries, mace, ground cinnamon, and chopped gingerroot
- 15 drops frankincense essential oil
- 10 drops myrrh essential oil

Parlor Potpourri

When it's ready, transfer the potpourri into small decorative containers and place on tables, shelves, or any other place it will be visually appreciated.

- ¾ cup noniodized salt
- ¼ cup *each* whole cloves, allspice berries, brown sugar, and crushed bay leaves
- 1 cup *each* rose petals and hydrangea petals
- ½ cup *each* dried rose geranium leaves, lavender flowers, and dried and crumbled rosemary sprigs
- ¼ cup *each* crushed bay leaves and orrisroot
- 2 tablespoons cognac

1. Combine the salt, cloves, allspice, brown sugar, and bay leaves in a bowl. In a separate bowl, mix the remaining ingredients except the cognac. Place some of this mixture in a widemouthed jar or crock and sprinkle with some of the salt mixture. Continue alternating layers in this manner, ending with a layer of the salt mixture.

2. Sprinkle the cognac over all and place a heavy rock on top to weigh the mixture down. Tightly seal the jar or crock. Stir this mixture once a day for 4 to 6 weeks, replacing the weight each time. If the mixture dries out, add a bit more cognac.

Herbal Mists

It's really quite simple to have an herbal spray air freshener available for every room of your home. It's a lot of fun to create unique blends that help eliminate unpleasant odors while expressing the real you. As a bonus, some sprays can perform double duty. For instance, in the kitchen, a small spray bottle of distilled water and thyme essential oil can be used to tame pungent cooking odors and as a wash for fruits and vegetables. Spray the produce and gently scrub with a vegetable brush. Rinse well in clean water.

Decorative cobalt glass bottles are a great choice if the herbal mist will be in view. Of course, you can use almost any spray bottle or even a plant mister. Plastic bottles are a good choice for households with small children or animals; always be sure to keep the mixtures out of their reach.

To make your own herbal spray air freshener, first wash the container thoroughly. Then fill it with water (use distilled if it's also going to come in contact with human skin or foods; do not use the spray on skin within 12 hours of exposure to sun) and add 5 to 7 drops of an essential oil or combination of oils per 8 ounces of water. There are some suggested blends on the following page.

BLEND	INGREDIENTS
Country Spice	cinnamon, ginger, vanilla, bay
Spring Morning	lavender, rose, geranium, rosemary, sweet orange
Earthy	sage, thyme, cedar, patchouli, frankincense
Romance	vanilla, sandalwood, ylang ylang, jasmine, neroli, rose
Far East	patchouli, cedar, sandalwood, lime, coriander
Energizing	basil, lavender, orange, nutmeg, mint
Calming	bergamot, geranium, clary sage, chamomile, yarrow
Gardener's Paradise	lemon, orange, basil, thyme

Simple Sachets

Sachets made from dried herbs and flowers will keep your linens and clothing smelling sweet while keeping insects at bay. A sachet formula doesn't need to be complicated to be effective — just a few ingredients are all that's required. In fact, if you don't have any dried herbs or flowers available, you can stuff the sachet with a bit of moss or even polyester fill scented with essential oil.

Sachets can be made in just minutes by stitching a double-layered square of cheesecloth, muslin, or a scrap of fabric on three sides and tying with a ribbon. You can also make use of those socks that mysteriously return mateless from the laundry room; socks are ideal for making sachets to scent sneakers, boots, and shoes. These are some of my favorite ways to use sachets:

* Hang them in clothes closets or coat closets.
* Place them in dresser drawers.
* Use them to keep seasonal clothes fresh when being stored, such as in a trunk or storage closet.
* Put some in your sneakers, gardening shoes, or any other regularly used shoes.
* Tuck them under sheets and towels in the linen closet.

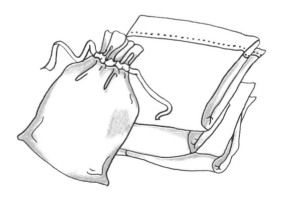

Spiced Sachets

This recipe has a zesty aroma and is especially nice to use around the holidays to scent linens for guests. You'll have enough filling for two to four sachets.

- 2 cups cinnamon chips
- ½ cup whole cloves
- ½ cup whole peppercorns
- ½ cup dried gingerroot slices
- 2 tablespoons ground cinnamon
- 1 tablespoon aniseed
- 2 teaspoons caraway seed

Combine all ingredients in a bowl and mix by hand or with a spoon to blend. Place spoonfuls of the blend onto muslin or cloth squares, leaving enough room to sew the sides together.

Deserving Drawers

This recipe is great to use in sock and sweater drawers. It lends a long-lasting earthy scent. Makes four to six sachets.

- 3 cups cedar chips
- 2 cups oakmoss
- 1 cup sandalwood chips
- 1 cup dried sage
- 1 vanilla bean, crushed
- 15 drops patchouli essential oil

Combine the cedar, oakmoss, sandalwood, and sage in a glass or ceramic bowl. Mix with a wooden spoon. Add the vanilla bean and patchouli oil and stir until completely mixed. Place spoonfuls of the blend onto muslin or cloth squares, leaving enough room to sew the sides together.

Sweet Linens Sachet

This sachet recipe imparts a sweet aroma to linens and towels. Remember, all herbal materials should be dried before using in sachets. Depending on the size of the squares, this recipe will make four to six sachets.

- **4   cups oakmoss**
- **2   cups rosemary leaves and flowers**
- **2   cups lavender leaves and flowers**
- **½   cup lemon balm or lemon verbena**
- **1   tablespoon orrisroot**
- **8   drops lavender essential oil**
- **6   drops rosemary essential oil**

Combine the dried herbs in a glass or ceramic bowl. Add the orrisroot and stir with a wooden spoon. Add the essential oils and mix well. Place spoonfuls of the blend onto muslin or cloth squares, leaving enough room to sew the sides together. Place sachets on shelves or hang inside linen closets and cupboards.

Mentholated Sneaker Tamer

Here's another odor-absorbing recipe to make your sneakers less unruly. Be sure to use only dried herbs in your potpourris.

- **2** cups natural clay cat litter
- **1** cup baking soda
- **1** cup calendula flowers
- **1** cup peppermint or spearmint leaves
- **½** cup thyme leaves
- **10** drops peppermint essential oil
- **10** drops wintergreen essential oil
- **10** drops eucalyptus essential oil

Combine the cat litter and baking soda in a glass or ceramic bowl and mix with a wooden spoon. Add the herbs and mix again. Add the essential oils and blend. Place half of the mixture in each of two clean socks and tie the open ends shut. Place a stuffed sock in each sneaker overnight or when not in use.

Sage Citrus Sneaker Tamer

If your sneakers advertise the fact that you've been working hard, this recipe will help you keep the news to yourself.

- **2** cups dried sage
- **1½** cups dried lemon balm
- **2** cups cedar chips
- **½** cup baking soda
- **2** tablespoons grated orange rind
- **10** drops rosemary essential oil
- **5** drops lemon essential oil

Combine the dried herbs, cedar chips, baking soda, and orange rind in a glass or ceramic bowl. Stir with a wooden spoon. Add the essential oils and stir to blend. Place half of the mixture in a clean sock and tie the open end shut. Stuff another sock with the remaining mixture and tie off. Place a stuffed sock in each sneaker overnight or when not in use.

More Fragrant Ideas

Don't limit yourself to the three main types of air fresheners discussed here — be creative!

Hang dried herbs in closets and storage rooms to deter insects. Some good choices are mints, rosemary, lavender, sage, lemongrass, and citronella.

Make vacuuming a sweeter experience: place a few drops of essential oil on the outside of the filter bag of your vacuum cleaner.

If you have a fireplace, place two or three drops of essential oil of choice on the wood before lighting.

Add a few drops of a citrus essential oil to your humidifier. Do not use essential oils for this purpose if you suffer from asthma, however.

Add one or two drops of essential oil to the rings made to attach to the bulb of a standing lamp. The heat of the bulb will release the fragrance when the lamp is in use. Don't allow the essential oil to come in direct contact with the bulb; this can cause the bulb to explode and could result in a fire.

CHAPTER 9

THE GARAGE & BASEMENT

THE GARAGE AND BASEMENT are two places where one is most likely to find the largest collection of solvents, paints, and various household chemicals. How do you safely and responsibly dispose of them?

The first rule of greening your garage and basement is to know what not to do. Do not, under any circumstances, pour these products down the drain, dump them outside, or send them to the landfill. Doing any of these things would be detrimental to the local groundwater and wildlife, as well as home septic systems.

The next step is to find out if your town or city has a collection program for hazardous waste materials. Your refuse and recycling collection provider may be able to provide this information, or have a program of its own. If you need more help, check out the Earth911.org website, where you can learn how to dispose of everything from automotive products to electronics just by entering your zip code.

Walls & Floors

You may think it's silly to clean the walls and floors of a garage or basement, but these areas can take on unpleasant odors and invading pathogens such as mold and mildew. And if the garage or basement is used for recreation or work, you'll especially appreciate the removal of these unwelcome visitors. The following formulas are made from simple ingredients and they are as effective as they are easy to use.

Mold & Mildew Destroyer

This formula works well on concrete floors and walls made of cinder block. Try it out in your garage or your basement. **Note:** *A string mop works best on cinder block walls because their texture tends to tear sponge mop heads.*

- ½ gallon water
- 2 cups hot vinegar
- 1 cup lemon juice
- 2 teaspoons tea tree essential oil

Combine all ingredients in a large bucket. Dip a mop into the bucket and wring out excess liquid. Wipe walls from the top down. Do not rinse. You can also wash concrete floors with this solution. If there are windows in the room, open them and let everything air-dry for a few hours.

Oil Spill Remover

If you're fortunate enough to be able to park your car in the garage, then one thing is certain: You will have occasional oil leaks or spills on the garage floor. Try this trick to remove the oil and its telltale odor.

- 2 cups natural cat litter or dry concrete mix
- ½ cup baking soda
- 8 drops eucalyptus or peppermint essential oil

Combine all ingredients in a small bucket or pail. Sprinkle mixture over the oil spill and let stand for 2 to 3 days. Then just sweep up the powder.

Helpful Hints for Storage Areas

Remove stale smells from freezers and ice chests by wiping the interior walls with equal parts water and white vinegar, followed by a second wipe with a clean cloth sprinkled with a few drops of essential oil of your choice, or vanilla extract.

Control excessive moisture in your basement by setting out a few bowls of charcoal pellets (not barbeque charcoal bricks). If you can't find charcoal pellets, clay or kitty litter will work, too.

Clean up mildewed books by sprinkling cornstarch that has been mixed with 1 to 2 drops of tea tree essential oil on the soiled pages. After a few hours, wipe the pages clean with a dry cloth.

Caring for Tools

To keep garden tools in good working order, they should be clean and dry before storing. Use a wire brush to remove dirt, and wipe tools with a dry cloth if they have any mud or moisture on them.

Tool Conditioner

Large tools like shovels and rakes should be stored in this mixture to prevent rusting.

1   quart olive oil
bucket of sand

Mix the olive oil into a bucket full of sand. Push large tools head first into the mixture and leave there when not in use.

SOUTH OF THE BORDER RUST REMOVER

Here's a simple, fragrant and nontoxic way to remove rust from your tools.

Sprinkle table salt directly on the tool, covering the rusty area completely. Sprinkle the juice from a freshly cut lime over the salt until saturated. Find something else to do for about three hours, then come back and wipe the rust-free tool clean.

Helpful Hints for Tool Maintenance

A peg board is a big tool-storing help in the garage. And if you outline your tools on the board with a pencil, you'll know when and what is missing.

Paint the handles of your tools a bright color, such as yellow or red. That way they'll be seen before they're stepped on or hit by the lawn mower.

Old tools can be recycled by turning them into garden ornaments. I use an old push broom handle to support a weather vane in one of my flower gardens. Antique tools can be displayed as a collection on the wall of a den or workshop. Just use your imagination!

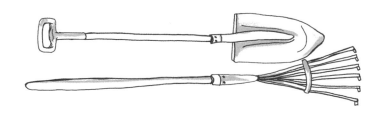

Clean Your Car Naturally

Even your automobiles can be cared for without the use of the toxic products currently sold for this purpose. The following formulas can be applied to your car, truck, boat, or recreational vehicle. Wear protective gloves when using these mixtures.

Easy Citrus Car Wash

This extremely simple formula is all you need to get your car clean.

- **1** **gallon water**
- **¼** **cup liquid castile soap**
- **10 drops lemon or orange essential oil**

Fill a bucket with the water and soap and stir until mixed. Add the essential oil and stir again. Using a soft cloth or sponge, wash the exterior of your car from the top down, one section at a time. Rinse each area well with clean water before the soap has a chance to dry.

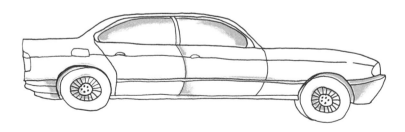

Get-Tough-to-Get-Dirt-Going Formula

This formula is for added shine and to remove really tough dirt and grime.

- **1 gallon water**
- **½ cup lemon juice**
- **6 drops eucalyptus or mint essential oil**
- **¼ cup liquid castile soap**
- **3 tablespoons baking soda**

Mix the water, lemon juice, essential oil, and soap in a bucket. Add the baking soda and stir until blended. With a soft cloth or sponge, wash the exterior of your car from the top down, working in sections. Rinse each area well with clean water before the soap dries.

Tire Wash

Use this cleaner to keep your tires looking like new.

- **2 cups baking soda**
- **½ cup water**
- **¼ cup liquid castile soap**
- **2 cups vinegar or lemon juice**
- **5 drops lemon, lime, or orange essential oil**

Combine the baking soda, water, and soap in a bucket or other container. Add the vinegar and essential oil, and mix well. Apply with a brush to get in between the tire treads. Wash one tire at a time, rinsing each before moving on to the next.

Headlight Scrub

This formula will easily remove grime and the remains of insects that have met their end on your headlights.

- ¼ cup baking soda
- 1½ tablespoons liquid castile soap
- 8 drops eucalyptus or pine essential oil

Combine all ingredients in a plastic bowl and mix well. Dip a cloth, brush, or sponge into the wash and scrub each headlight. Rinse several times with a wet cloth or sponge or with a garden hose.

Herbal Car Wax

An all–natural recipe, this wax really protects your car's finish. It can be made in larger quantities and stored.

- 3 tablespoons beeswax
- 3 tablespoons carnauba wax
- 1 cup linseed oil
- 6 drops orange or lemon essential oil
- ½ cup lemon juice

1. Melt waxes and linseed oil together in a double boiler, stirring often. Add the essential oil, stir once, and immediately remove from heat.
2. Pour the mixture into a clean coffee can. (*Note:* The can will become hot.) Using gloves or potholders, place the coffee can in a place where it will be undisturbed for a few days.

3. When the wax has completely hardened, tap the sides out of the can until the wax breaks free. Turn out the wax and rub it directly on your car.

4. Dip a soft cloth into the lemon juice and squeeze dry. Polish the waxed car with the lemon juice–soaked cloth, then buff to a shine with a dry cloth.

Fresh-Scent Vinyl Upholstery Cleaner

If you're sensitive to that new car smell, this formula will help eliminate it.

2	tablespoons baking soda
2	cups hot water
1	teaspoon orange, cedar, or mint essential oil

Dissolve baking soda in hot water. Blend in essential oil. Vacuum the upholstery to remove loose dirt and debris from crevices and between the seats. (Watch out for loose change!) Moisten a soft cloth with the formula and rub over the upholstery, working from the top down. Rinse with a clean, damp cloth then dry to a shine with a dry towel.

Lavender Leather Upholstery Cleaner

To safely clean leather and impart a light lavender scent, try this formula. After cleaning, apply Fragrant Leather Upholstery Conditioner (facing page).

¼ cup soap flakes

1 cup hot water

6 drops mint or lavender essential oil

Dissolve soap flakes in hot water. Add essential oil and blend. Apply this formula with a soft brush, using gentle downward strokes. Wipe with a clean, damp cloth. Buff dry with a towel.

Old-Fashioned Cloth Upholstery Cleaner

This old-time recipe really works!

2 cups water

¼ cup dried soapwort root or ¾ cup fresh stems

1. If using the dried root, soak it in the 2 cups of water overnight. If using fresh material, chop the stems into 1-inch pieces.

2. Bring the soapwort and water to a boil for 1 minute. Reduce heat and simmer for 20 minutes, stirring occasionally. Remove from heat and let the decoction stand until cool. Strain, and the cleaner is ready to use.

3. Dip a cloth or brush into the cleaner and rub into the upholstery using a downward motion. Rinse with a clean, damp cloth. Allow the upholstery to air-dry.

Fragrant Leather Upholstery Conditioner

Use this conditioner after cleaning your leather upholstery with Lavender Leather Upholstery Cleaner (facing page). The olive oil and rosemary tea will keep leather seats soft and conditioned.

½ **cup olive oil**
¼ **cup strong rosemary tea**
¼ **cup vinegar**

Combine all ingredients in a plastic spray bottle and shake well. Lightly spray onto upholstery and buff with a dry cloth.

Quick Chrome Cleaner

If there are a lot of stains or bugs stuck on the chrome parts of your car, you can use a nylon-backed sponge with this formula. Make your own nylon sponge by securing a square of onion bag netting over a clean sponge or cloth. Note: *Use a plastic squirt bottle for this recipe, since the mixture may clog the nozzle of a spray bottle.*

½ **cup baking soda**
¼ **cup lemon juice**
3 **drops citrus essential oil of choice**

Combine baking soda and lemon juice in a plastic squirt bottle. Add the essential oil and shake well. Apply directly to chrome and wipe with a damp cloth. Rinse with clean water.

Dashboard Restorer

This simple formula will make your dashboard look brand new again.

1 cup water
½ cup vegetable oil–based soap (such as Murphy's)
10 drops cedar essential oil

Combine all ingredients in a small plastic spray bottle and shake well. Spray onto dashboard and wipe clean with a soft cloth.

Tar Solvent

This formula is for those specks of tar that land on your car after driving on a freshly paved road.

1 tablespoon lemon juice or vinegar
2 teaspoons lemon essential oil
4 drops tea tree essential oil

Mix all ingredients in a small bowl. Rub some of the solution into tar with glove-protected fingertips or a sponge to loosen. Allow the formula to remain on the tar for 15 minutes, then wipe or scrape the remaining tar off with a nylon-backed sponge.

Window Wash

In the winter, this formula helps reduce frost buildup.

- **3 cups vinegar**
- **1 cup water**
- **10 drops lemon essential oil**

Combine all ingredients in a large plastic spray bottle and shake well. Spray liberally onto windows and wipe clean with a chamois cloth.

Mat & Carpet Cleaner

Even if you've cleaned your car inside and out, dingy mats and carpeting will spoil the effect. This solution not only cleans the items, but also makes them smell fresh again.

- **½ gallon hot water**
- **½ cup liquid soap**
- **12 drops wintergreen or peppermint essential oil**

1. Combine all ingredients in a bucket or pail. Stir thoroughly to mix.
2. Vacuum loose dirt from carpeting and mats. Remove mats from the car and clean by dipping a brush into the cleaning solution and rubbing into the carpet fibers. Rinse the mats with a hose and allow them to dry in the sun.
3. Clean the carpeting on the floor of the car by dipping a brush into the cleaning solution and rubbing into the carpet. Wipe with a dry towel. Vacuum again when completely dry.

CLEANING SEASONAL VEHICLES

Here's a way to tackle musty odors from campers, boats, and motor homes that haven't been in use for long periods of time. Fill a small bowl with a little white vinegar and a few drops of essential oil, if you wish. Add a piece of bread on top of the liquid and place the bowl inside the vehicle to absorb odors. Remove the bowl after 24 hours.

Instant Herbal Car Deodorizer

If your pets frequently travel in the car, then you know how odors can linger long after the ride is over. This formula will eliminate those odors.

- ¾ cup water
- ¼ cup vinegar
- 6 drops lavender essential oil
- 4 drops lemon essential oil
- 4 drops sweet orange essential oil
- 2 drops peppermint essential oil

Combine all ingredients in a small plastic spray bottle (about 8 ounces) and shake well. Hold the spray bottle 6–8 inches from surfaces and lightly mist upholstery and carpeting. Leave the windows and doors open for 15 minutes after spraying, if possible. Don't let Fido back into the car immediately, as the essential oils can irritate his paws and sensitive nose.

Herbal Fragrance Pouch

You also can make this air-freshening pouch with a single larger piece of fabric gathered at the top with a piece of colorful ribbon.

2   squares of fabric, 4 x 4 inches each
1   square of cotton batting, 3 x 3 inches, or
        six cotton balls
5   drops cedar essential oil
5   drops patchouli essential oil
3   drops sandalwood essential oil
2   drops neroli (orange blossom) or sweet
        orange essential oil

1. Place one of the squares of fabric on a flat surface, pattern side down. On top of this place the cotton batting or cotton balls. Add the essential oils to the cotton and place the remaining square of fabric, pattern side up, on top.

2. Stitch or use a hot glue gun to seal the edges of the fabric squares. Attach a loop or strand of ribbon at the top and hang it from your rearview mirror.

Fruity Travel Wipes

These travel wipes are quick and easy to make. They sure come in handy, too!

- **10** drops lemon essential oil
- **4** drops grapefruit seed extract
- **6** drops lime essential oil
- **2** drops tea tree essential oil
- **10** squares cut from cellulose sponge cloth or cotton T-shirts, 5 x 8 inches each

1. Fold each square of cloth in half and place in a plastic zipper bag or a small plastic container with an airtight lid. Add enough water to saturate each cloth, but not enough to cover them.
2. Press down on the cloths with one hand and drain excess water into a cup. Add the remaining ingredients to the water and stir. Pour this mixture over the cloths once more and seal the container.
3. Keep in the glove compartment of your car and use when needed to clean hands and face.

Sudden Spill & Spot Remover

*It never fails — someone spills ice cream or soda on the floor or
upholstery just as you've pulled onto the highway. This formula
will lift out most stains, including those left by greasy foods, and
leave a fresh, clean smell.*

- ½ **cup vinegar**
- ½ **cup club soda**
- 8 **drops eucalyptus essential oil**
- 3 **drops wintergreen essential oil**

Combine all ingredients in a small plastic spray bottle and
shake well. Spray directly onto stain and blot with a clean, dry
cloth. Repeat as necessary.

EMERGENCY CARE FOR MOTION SICKNESS

If someone in your family is prone to car sickness, you don't want to be without this simple
remedy! Place 2 or 3 drops of peppermint or
ginger essential oil on a tissue. Sniff the tissue
until the feeling passes. Although this treatment usually works well for people, I can't be
sure about its effect on the family dog.

Under-the-Hood Maintenance

You didn't think you'd see any herbal formulas in this department, did you? In truth, there aren't many, but what is presented here is useful nonetheless. These formulas can be used on the engine of your car, lawn mower, or other machinery.

Engine Degreaser

A buildup of oil and grease on an engine can adversely affect performance, and could result in engine fire. Cut through grease with this powerful cleaner.

¼ cup washing soda

1 cup water

1 cup vinegar

25 drops tea tree essential oil

20 drops citrus essential oil of choice

1. Pour the washing soda into a plastic jug or pitcher, one with a tight-fitting cap and preferably a pour spout.

2. Bring the water and vinegar to a boil in a saucepan. Remove from heat and add to the pitcher. Cap the pitcher and shake to dissolve the washing soda. (Careful — it will be hot!) Add the essential oils and shake once more.

3. Slowly pour the solution over a cool engine (one that has not been run for at least an hour). Use a stiff brush to loosen oil and grease. Rinse with a garden hose or pour clean water over the engine several times. Leave the engine exposed to the air until completely dry.

Battery Terminal Cleaner

Battery terminals can develop a lot of gunk over time, leading to corrosion and a shortened life for your battery.

- ½   cup baking soda
- 4   drops lime or orange essential oil
- water to make a paste

Combine all ingredients in a small bowl or cup and blend well, using only enough water to make a paste of medium thickness. Apply the paste to battery terminals with an old toothbrush and scrub until clean. Wipe the terminals clean with a slightly damp cloth, then wipe again with a dry cloth.

Corrosion Resistance for Battery Terminals

To keep unsightly battery corrosion from happening, use this simple formula. **Note:** *The paintbrush you use can be restored by soaking it in hot vinegar.*

- ½   tablespoon 100% pure aloe vera gel
- 1   tablespoon petroleum jelly

Mix the aloe vera gel and petroleum jelly together in a cup. Apply the mixture to the battery terminals with the tip of a small paintbrush.

Radiator Rescue

This formula has two parts. Use the wash for the exterior of your car radiator, then follow with the finishing treatment to deter rust.

TO WASH:

2   cups boiling water

¾   cup washing soda

6   drops rosemary essential oil

TO FINISH:

1   cup water

2   teaspoons pure linseed oil

1. Combine wash ingredients in a bowl or other container; stir to mix. Pour over a cool radiator and use a brush to clean off any oil or grease residue.

2. Rinse with clean water and allow the radiator to air-dry.

3. Combine the finish ingredients in a small spray bottle and shake well. Lightly spray radiator. Allow to air-dry before using the vehicle.

GASKET & HOSE MAINTENANCE

Protect gaskets and hoses from cracking in extreme temperatures: Pour a few tablespoons of olive oil into a cup, then dip the tip of a small paintbrush into the oil and shake off any excess. Apply to rubber hoses and gaskets, and also door seals. Go over these areas again with a dry cloth to remove excess oil.

CHAPTER 10

THE GARDEN & LANDSCAPE

PERSONALLY, I regard my yard, deck, and gardens as extensions of my home, even though they are seasonal territories. And, because we have several "fur-kids" in the form of three cats herded by an Australian Shepherd, it is absolutely essential to maintain a safe and healthy outdoor environment.

Unfortunately, these outdoor living spaces can become vulnerable to unwelcome intrusions, including mildew on your outdoor accoutrements and pests in your plants. The good news is that it's perfectly possible to exercise as much care for the exterior of your home as the interior, and do it as naturally as possible to reduce your environmental impact.

From the following pages you'll discover how to make and use natural formulas to care for brick, decking, siding, wicker furniture, and even your outdoor grill. You'll also learn how to safely and effectively convince unwanted garden visitors to find greener pastures.

Decks, Patios & Exterior Siding

One of the easiest and most effective methods to clean these types of surfaces is a good washing with a pressure washer. However, if you don't have access to one, or have some tough stains that stubbornly remain even after power washing, then try one of these advanced solutions.

Replace plain water with equal parts water and white vinegar in your pressure washer. You may also add 1 tablespoon of powdered citric acid for each cup of liquid, if you wish.

Oxalic acid is an organic substance that occurs naturally in many plants, most notably tea (*Camellia sinensis*), sorrel, buckwheat, and rhubarb, as well as in most berries and certain fruits. Used to bleach wood decking and remove mildew, rust, and other stains, it is available from most hardware stores and home centers as dry crystals that are reconstituted in water. However, being a caustic acid it's also highly corrosive, and great care should be taken to protect your skin and eyes, as well as taking precautions to prevent children and pets from coming into contact with this material.

If working with oxalic acid doesn't appeal to you (and you don't mind spending a little more), Napier Environmental Technologies offers many types of water-based, nonsolvent products under the brand name of Bio-Wash, including washes, stains, and treatments for wood, concrete, vinyl siding, and fiberglass. (See Resources.)

Wicker Furniture

Wicker refers to the art of weaving a variety of plant-based fibers to lend form and structure, a practice that dates back to ancient Egypt. The base material may be wood, vine, or rush. As furniture, wicker is durable yet light, making it very portable and suitable décor for porches, covered patios, and sun rooms.

Today, some so-called wicker furnishings are actually made from plastic, and if your outdoor furniture is, cleaning it is an easy task. An occasional wipe down with a damp cloth is all that's needed. However, other types of wicker require a different method of cleaning. For instance, wood and vine-based wicker needs some humidity to keep it from cracking, while wicker made from paper fiber rush cannot tolerate moisture at all. For this reason, try to determine what kind of wicker you have. If you can't, or if your wicker is painted, then stick to cleaning it with a vacuum hose, or a dry cloth.

Weekend Warrior Wicker Wash

If you know that your wicker is wood-based, you can go to town cleaning it with this formula without being concerned about getting it wet. The essential oils used here will dissolve grime, while the gentle soap will make its removal easier.

1   gallon of water
1   tablespoon liquid castile soap (or Murphy's Oil Soap)
20 drops cedar essential oil
10 drops sweet orange oil

Combine all ingredients in a pail of water. Dip a soft cloth or cellulose sponge into the cleaning solution, squeeze out the excess liquid, and wipe down the wicker using even strokes from top to bottom. Wipe a second time with a clean, dry cloth. Let the furniture dry completely before using it again, usually for several hours.

Lemony Wicker Conditioning Treatment

This technique may be used to restore wood- or vine-based wicker.

1½ cups hot water
20 drops lemon essential oil
¼   cup flaxseed oil (also known as linseed)

Combine the hot water and lemon essential oil in a spray bottle and gently shake to mix. Apply this solution to clean wicker and allow the item to dry in the sun. When dry, apply a very light coating of flaxseed oil using a clean, dry cloth. After a day or two, the oil will be absorbed. If any residue remains, simply wipe the wicker with a dry cloth before using the furniture again.

BOTTOM'S UP TIP FOR WICKER

Sometimes, wicker seats can sag with age and frequent use. To remedy this, spray the wicker (wood or rattan only) completely with plain water. Then set the furniture in the sun to dry. This will help the wicker bands to tighten.

Cleaning Stone & Brick

Dirt, spills, grease, and soot can affect the function and appearance of stone and brick objects, such as barbeque pits, retaining walls, patio flooring, and chimeneas (freestanding fireplaces). Here's how to keep these items looking and performing at their best.

TERRA-COTTA CARE TIPS

* Put a coffee filter (preferably unbleached) in the bottom of your terra-cotta pots before planting to prevent soil loss and staining of your deck flooring and railings.
* Place small seashells in pots, upside down, to help capture and retain moisture between watering.
* To help keep terra-cotta pots looking clean and new, coat them inside and out with a light layer of flaxseed or olive oil.

Give Up the Grime Degreaser

Washing soda is a natural degreaser and camphor essential oil is employed as a solvent in the paint industry. If you can't find this essential oil at your local health food store, look for an online supplier (see Resources). It's very inexpensive and a little goes a long way.

- 1 gallon hot water
- ½ cup washing soda
- 30 drops white camphor essential oil

Combine all ingredients in a pail or bucket. Dip a scrub brush into the cleaning solution and apply to the brick or stone surface and scrub (wearing gloves is recommended). Once the entire surface has been cleaned, rinse thoroughly with a garden hose.

Barbeque Grills

Stainless Steel Barbeque Polish

Wipe this solution on your barbeque's exterior for lots of shine.

- ½ cup water
- 4–5 teaspoons baking soda
- 10 drops lavender essential oil

Combine the water and just enough baking soda to make a thin paste—it should be goopy, not too thick. Add the essential oil and blend well. Apply the paste onto your barbeque using circular motions with a soft cloth. Rinse with either plain water, or a solution of equal parts water and white vinegar. Finish by drying and buffing the stainless steel with a dry cloth.

Pest-free Garden Parties

Once you've cleaned your deck, your outdoor furniture, and your grill, you'll want to enjoy your yard without being bugged by bugs. To keep ants from spoiling your picnic, sprinkle a mixture of salt and ground cinnamon around the area. If your bug problems are in the air rather than on the ground, hang strips of ribbon or cloth that have been moistened with several drops of lavender essential oil from nearby trees or other stationary fixtures to deter flying insects. Other natural fly repellents include placing a bowl of lemon or orange peels on the table, or using the Shoo-Fly Shake below.

Shoo-Fly Shake

Place a few small bowls filled with the following combination of dried herbs outside to keep flies away from your backyard barbeque or afternoon tea party.

- 2 cups lavender flowers
- 1 cup rosemary
- 1 cup southernwood
- ½ cup spearmint
- ¼ cup mugwort
- ¼ cup cedarwood chips
- 3 heaping tablespoons orrisroot

Combine all ingredients.

Pest Patrol & Control

Pests come in an assorted variety — some with roots and others with tails; some may be merely bothersome, while others can be downright destructive. All of them can affect your enjoyment of your outdoor landscape. Worse yet, some of these pests need to be dealt with outside before they have the opportunity to take up residence inside your home.

Before you can control common pests, you must first patrol to see where your home and property may be vulnerable to entry. Cracks around windows and doors should be sealed. If you find any holes intended for electrical or plumbing coming into the house that a mouse or other creature could slip into, fill up the excess space with steel wool. Inspect your garden plants, trees, and shrubs for signs of unwelcome visitors, such as aphids or fungus. Once you've completed your rounds and taken notes, you'll be ready to take control of your outdoor living space.

Struggling with Weeds

What distinguishes a weed from a valid garden plant is a personal choice for each gardener. Some people deliberately harvest and even cultivate dandelions, for instance, to make dandelion wine or fritters (try them both sometime!). Others consider this prolific plant to be a pesky nuisance. In any case, you'll want to refrain from using toxic chemicals to prevent any unwanted flora from encroaching upon your lawn or garden areas.

Corn gluten, a by-product from corn milling, is the latest newcomer to organic lawn care controls and is valued for its effectiveness as both a lawn food and a weed deterrent. Corn gluten works as a natural plant food because it delivers nitrogen. At the same time, however, it prevents germination of invading weeds by robbing the seed of moisture as soon as it sprouts. This preemergent ability not only helps to rid your lawn of dandelions, but also some of the most persistent invaders, such as purslane and crabgrass.

Corn gluten is available as a fine powder, as pellets, or in granular form, the latter being the easiest to distribute via a spreader. Some garden centers carry this product in stock. However, some of you may need to order it online. In either case, be sure to follow the directions on the package to ensure proper application and watering to activate this double duty weed and feed.

Homemade Herbal Herbicide

This formula is highly effective at eradicating unwanted lawn and garden dwellers, including poison ivy. However, it will also kill any plant that comes in contact with it, so be careful where you spray it. Note: *Herbal extracts are not the same thing as essential oils. Extracts are liquids that are distilled from raw plant material using alcohol. See Resources for suppliers.*

- 2 **cups white vinegar**
- ½ **cup salt**
- ¼ **cup powdered citric acid**
- ¼ **cup witch hazel extract**
- 2 **teaspoons lavender extract**
- 2 **teaspoons chamomile extract**
- ¼ **cup wheat germ oil**

1. Heat the white vinegar in a medium saucepan until it just comes to a boil. (You might want to open the windows first.)
2. Remove from heat and add the salt, stirring well to dissolve. Add the remaining ingredients, and stir again.
3. Using a funnel, pour the solution into a large plastic spray bottle.
4. Spray the solution directly onto the weed, including the base near the roots. If possible, try to apply the solution while it's still hot for best results.

Horsetail Garden Tea

Horsetail is abundant in silica, making this herb's properties beneficial to garden plants as a nutrient, as well as being an excellent deterrent for mildew and other fungi.

- **1 gallon of water**
- **1 cup dried horsetail (leaves and stems)**

Bring the water to a boil, and then add the dried horsetail. Reduce to a simmer and brew for 20 minutes. Strain and pour the reserved infusion into a plastic spray bottle. Allow the solution to cool completely before spraying liberally on and around your plants.

Got Milky Spore?

This excellent organic product solves several problems at once and will keep on working for up to 40 years! Milky Spore is a naturally occurring friendly bacteria for lawns. This natural treatment is lethal to grubs, which are actually the larvae of Japanese Beetles, a common and harmful garden pest that feeds on grass, flowers, fruits — just about anything that grows out of the ground. By getting rid of the grubs, you'll not only be reducing the Japanese Beetle population; you will also be removing the primary food source for another destructive visitor — the mole. Best of all, Milky Spore won't harm the surrounding soil, grass, or your children and pets.

You might be able to find this product at your local garden center. If not, check for an online supplier (see Resources). It's not very expensive and it goes a long way — a 10-ounce container will cover about 2,500 square feet. The spores continue to self-propagate, too, even lying dormant over long periods of time until an unsuspecting grub enters the scene. This endurance is why it's so effective for so long.

Friendly Fungicides

While not exactly friendly to pests and disease, there are some organic elementals and minerals that are far less toxic than standard pesticides and fungicides. If you have a severe problem with black spot or powdery mildew running rampant among your plants, however, you might want to consider using one of these materials.

Keep in mind that even though the following agents may be naturally occurring, that doesn't mean you don't need to exercise caution while using them. With that said, make sure that you follow all package directions and recommended precautions very carefully.

Copper sulfate, colloidal sulfate, and elemental sulfur are all accepted by organic gardening standards and are very effective against forms of mildew, black spot, damp-off (a viral disease that affects seedlings), arthropods, and mites. These materials work by altering the pH on the surface of the vegetation, rendering it unsuitable to sustain fungal growth. In addition, these agents disrupt the metabolic processes of insects, which inhibits reproduction. *Caution:* Sulfur and sulfur compounds are corrosive to metal.

Diatomaceous Earth (DE) is applied as a powder, which is composed of crushed fossils. Nontoxic to humans, DE keeps the population levels of many lawn residents in check, such as grubs, slugs, and fleas. One caveat: DE will also kill beneficial insects on your lawn, such as nematodes. For this reason, you may only want to use DE in the infested area rather than broadcast it across the entire lawn.

Pyrethrum is a natural pesticide made from certain species of the chrysanthemum family that are native to Africa. Its active constituents, pyrethrins and cinerins, are highly effective against aphids, spider mites, and a variety of other leaf-chomping pests. It's also safe and environmentally friendly, since it goes to work quickly and then readily biodegrades in sunlight. In fact, this substance can be applied right up until the time vegetables are harvested and can even be used indoors. Cons: Pyrethrum is toxic to pond fish until it has a chance to biodegrade. Also, pyrethrum-based formulas (it is sometimes combined with neem) should not be confused with pyrethroid insecticides. The latter is an entirely different composition and is quite toxic to humans and animals.

All-Natural Plant Protection

Many DIY insecticides can be made without making a trip to the garden center. For large gardens, double the recipe and use quart- or gallon-size sprayers. In addition, you may need to reapply these solutions after a heavy rain.

Tea Tree & GSE Fungal Fighter

Diseases such as mildews and fungi can easily be transferred from plant to plant, or even different sections of the same plant when they hop onto pruning sheers as the vehicle. Spray your sheers with this simple formula to prevent this from happening.

- **2 cups water**
- **10 drops grapefruit seed extract (GSE)**
- **10 drops tea tree essential oil**

Combine all ingredients into a large plastic spray bottle. Shake well before using on shears. After spraying, wait 2–3 minutes before wiping dry with a clean cloth.

All-Natural Aphid Spray

Aphids, also known as plant lice or blackfly, can quickly destroy foliage and spread disease. However, the oils, salts, and acids found in this formula will send them packing just as fast.

- **1 cup water**
- **1 cup white vinegar**
- **½ cup salt**

- ¼ cup powdered citric acid
- ¼ cup baking soda
- 2 teaspoons aloe vera juice
- 2 teaspoons sesame seed oil
- 15 drops sage essential oil
- 10 drops grapefruit seed extract

Combine all ingredients into a large plastic spray bottle. Shake before using and be sure to apply to the underside of leaves where aphids love to hide.

Get Going Garlic Spray

This formula is effective for most insects, including ants, if sprayed along their routes of travel that are bringing them to your door.

- ½ cup flaxseed oil
- 5–6 garlic cloves, smashed with skins on
- 2 cups water
- 1 teaspoon liquid castile soap

Combine the flaxseed oil and garlic cloves in a bowl. Cover and let sit overnight. Meanwhile, add the remaining ingredients to a large plastic spray bottle. Strain the garlic from the flaxseed oil, and then add the reserved oil to the bottle. Shake well before using.

You Say Potato, I Say Tomato

Natural insecticides made from potato starch and tea brewed from leaves of the tomato plant are both age–old methods of pest control. This formula brings both together for an extra kick. The result is especially effective against white cabbage butterflies in the vegetable garden.

6½ cups of water

2　tablespoons potato flour

1½ cups fresh tomato leaves, packed

1　teaspoon liquid castile soap

10 drops peppermint essential oil

1. Bring 6 cups of the water to a boil in a medium saucepan. Add the tomato leaves and stir.
2. Remove from heat, cover, and steep for 30 minutes. Strain off the tomato leaves, reserving the liquid.
3. Add the potato flour to the remaining ½ cup of water and blend well (just like you're making gravy). Add the flour mixture to the tomato leaf tea.
4. Add the castile soap and peppermint essential oil, stir, and pour into a large plastic spray bottle.

Classic Cayenne Pepper Spray

Since many common garden pests are soft-bodied, they will avoid coming into contact with strong irritants such as onion, garlic, and cayenne pepper. As a bonus, simply omit the soap from this formula, and you've got a great seasoning for a Cajun meal!

1   small onion
4–5 cloves of garlic, skins on
olive oil
1   teaspoon cayenne pepper
2   cups water
1   teaspoon liquid castile soap

Using a blender or food processor, make a pulp out of the onion and garlic cloves. Spoon the pulp into a small bowl or cup and add just enough olive oil to cover. Let this mixture rest overnight. In the morning, strain off the olive oil and add the cayenne pepper. Keep this mixture in a glass jar on a shelf for a few days. When ready to use in the garden, add 1 teaspoon of the cayenne–olive oil blend to a large bottle filled with the water and the castile soap. Shake well before applying.

Of Mice & Moles

Certain plants seem to chase off moles before they can start burrowing into your lawn and uproot your flowers, such as: all alliums (such as garlic, onions, leeks, and chives), daffodil, and Mexican marigold. Castor bean and caper spurge (dubbed "the mole plant") are also effective, but beware: these plants are poisonous and may not be suitable if small children or pets are present.

Mice don't care for peppermint very much and tend to avoid areas where it grows. Keeping a few potted peppermint plants near the foundation of your home, or giving this mint a place in your culinary herb garden, will help to deter them from making their home in yours. If mice seem to be checking out your weekly trash, try adding a few cot-ton balls moistened with a few drops of peppermint essential oil to the top of the garbage heap.

Deterring Deer

Deer can be a chronic problem for us country dwellers. They're very persistent — and cunning. Deer have an ability to sprint over fences that rivals an Olympic Triathlon Gold Medalist. They have long memories, too, and always remember where to find a free meal. Fortunately, they can be persuaded to pass up the menu in your garden if you know what they don't like to eat. The big turn off seems to be any form of decaying animal protein. Smelly? Yes. Effective? Very.

MORE NATURAL DEER GUARDS
Make use of thick or thorny shrubbery in your landscaping, such as barberry. Deer won't be so attracted to your yard if they can't see into it, plus a tough thicket is uncomfortable to pass through. Many gardeners report that a few

rows of wormwood planted around the perimeter of a property will also turn deer away. When ordering plants from catalogs, look for a deer-resistant rating associated with your selections.

Deer Be Gone

This formula will deter deer from eating your prized shrubbery, ground covers, and other plantings. You can also spray this mixture around the perimeter of your property (it can be doubled, of course) to help keep them from wandering onto your grounds at all. Note that a heavy rain will necessitate reapplication. Otherwise, it should be reapplied every 2–3 weeks.

- 1 cup buttermilk (or regular milk soured with a tablespoon of white vinegar)
- 3 whole eggs, lightly beaten and strained through a sifter
- 1 teaspoon liquid castile soap
- 1 teaspoon olive oil
- 1 tablespoon Tabasco sauce
- 25 drops clove essential oil
- 1 gallon of water, 2 cups removed

Blend all ingredients exept the water in a blender or food processor. Using a funnel, pour the mixture into the water (1 gallon, minus 2 cups). Cap the container and shake well. With a sprayer, apply the mixture to tops of the plants or the ground you wish to protect. The surface should be lightly sprayed, not saturated.

Keep Pets Out of Flowerbeds

If Fido is unearthing your prized tulips, or if Fluffy thinks your rose garden is her outdoor litter box, then you need this simple solution. You can double the recipe if you have a large garden or more than one flowerbed.

Out Spot Formula

This scent of this mixture is usually enough to turn your pet away from your flowerbeds. However, you may need to reapply this mixture after a heavy rain or watering.

- ½ cup all-purpose flour
- 3 tablespoons dry mustard
- 1 tablespoon powdered cayenne pepper

Combine all ingredients in a bowl or paper bag. Sprinkle this mixture liberally on the borders of your flower beds, reapplying as necessary.

CHAPTER
11

THE HOME OFFICE

MORE THAN FOUR MILLION PEOPLE IN NORTH AMERICA
work from home on a daily basis, while almost as many
telecommute at least part-time. Many homes are now
equipped with fully functional home offices, where the
same germs and grime appear as in traditional office
settings. In fact, the only difference between these two
locations is the absence of a water cooler in the former
and piles of laundry begging for attention in the latter.

The formulas and suggestions found in this chapter
address equipment common to both. They can also
extend to other environments we find ourselves sta-
tioned in for significant periods of time, such as hotels,
school, day-care facilities, and college dormitories. To
that end, consider this chapter a keep-it-clean-and-
green guide when home is where you work, or when
your home is temporarily away from home.

Why Clean Computer Equipment?

Keeping your home office computer and related equipment clean not only reduces the spread of germs in this often-shared space (what family with kids has a home office that isn't used to do homework, download music, and play video games?), but will also extend the life of the components. In fact, computer lock-ups and erratic mouse movements can be prevented by routine maintenance. Dust, environmental pollutants, and pet hair can build up inside these items and clog the works. The technical term for this event is known as *entropy*, and it occurs when household dust naturally gravitates to heat sinks and casings, which serve to pull heat away from sensitive circuitry. If these parts become excessively dirty, a malfunction is sure to follow.

The ABCs of Cleaning CPUs

The CPU (central processing unit) is that big box that everything else gets plugged into and is the most important component to care for. Actually, the CPU is the computer — everything else is an add-on peripheral device. Fortunately, you don't need to know anything about computer parts to clean the CPU's interior. All you need is a clean, dry cotton cloth, a few cotton swabs, some rubbing alcohol, a vacuum, and a can of compressed air.

Basically, a good cleaning of the inside of the CPU involves removing the cover and looking for excessive dirt and dust. If you find some, use the can of compressed air to dislodge it and remove it with the vacuum cleaner. Also, check for and remove any lint trapped in the dust filter (in some models, this filter is removable for thorough cleaning), as well as in and around the fan and air vents. If you discover any gunk buildup on major surfaces (avoid circuits), carefully clean it off with a cotton swab dabbed in a tiny bit of rubbing alcohol.

That's it; you're done. Plan to repeat this interior cleaning twice a year, more often if you have pets.

Basic Office Dust- & Germ-Buster

Use this formula to clean the outer surfaces of your office equipment, such as the keyboard, monitor (but avoid the glass), printer, and fax machine.

2	cups water
1	cup white vinegar
1	teaspoon grapefruit seed extract
10	drops sweet orange essential oil

Combine all ingredients in a plastic spray bottle and shake well. Spray directly onto a dry cloth and wipe surfaces clean.

Keyboards

If you tend to snack while you work, there are probably a lot of crumbs lodged in between the keys of your keyboard, which can cause the keys to stop working. Even if you don't eat over the keyboard, it's remarkable how filthy the keys can become over time simply from the oils from your fingers. The remedy for both is to clean the top of each key with a soft cloth moistened with rubbing alcohol or tea tree essential oil and use a cotton swab to get in between keys, if necessary. Either substance will safely and effectively remove built up grime and kill germs.

If you spill a liquid onto a keyboard, immediately shut off the computer. Then unplug the keyboard and turn it upside down over some towels and allow it to dry out for at least 24 hours. Clean off what sticky residue you can on the outer surface and then see if it will work when you plug it in again. If not, you'll be getting a new keyboard.

Easy Breezy Glass Cleaner

The monitor screen and the glass surfaces of fax and copier machines can take on a lot of fingerprints and smudges, or what I call "schmutz." Keep this simple cleaner nearby to keep these surfaces schmutz free.

- **1 cup water**
- **1 cup white vinegar**
- **10 drops lemon or lime essential oil**

Combine all ingredients in a small plastic spray bottle and shake a few times to blend. Spray lightly onto a cleaning cloth and wipe surfaces until dry. Shake before each use.

When Cleaning Electronics

Use cotton to clean surfaces since it doesn't produce static electricity like other materials.

Spray cleaning solutions on the cleaning cloth, not on the component.

Compressed air (or gas) is relatively benign, but make sure the can is recyclable.

It's okay to clean the outer workings of mouse wheels or even disk drives with rubbing alcohol and a cotton swab, but stay away from circuitry.

All-Purpose Cleaning Wipes

With these easy-to-make wipes on hand, keeping your home office fresh and free of germs is just a pop-up away. The basil essential oil is not only antiseptic, but it's also stimulating and may help to increase productivity. You can also reuse the cloths after cleaning them in the normal cycle of the dishwasher.

- **1 cup water**
- **1 cup vinegar**
- **15 drops basil essential oil**
- **cotton or microfiber cloth**

Cut the cloth into small squares or rectangles and stack them on top of each other (10 is a good number). Pour the water, vinegar and basil essential oil into a heavy-duty plastic bag with a zipper closure. Close the bag and gently squeeze to blend the ingredients. Place your stacked cloth pieces into the bag and close the bag again, pressing down to squeeze out excess air. Use these wipes for quick cleanups, making sure to squeeze out the excess liquid from each wipe first. (*Note:* Not recommended for nonsealed wood.)

Perk Up Office Plants

Keeping plants in your working space offers visual appeal as well as serving as living air purifiers. Here are some suggestions on how to keep these — and even artificial flowers and plants — in good shape.

Unusual but true, milk is actually a great substance to clean dust from plant leaves and give them a beautiful shine. Dip a soft, clean cloth into ½ cup of whole or 2 percent milk (use more or less depending on how many plants you have). Squeeze out the excess liquid, and then proceed to wipe plant leaves clean. Be careful not to let any of the milk pool on the leaves or you'll end up with spots. *Note:* A sock worn over the hand in place of a cloth is perfect for this task.

Cleaning silk or fabric floral arrangements can be tricky since the assembly and components may not hold up to liquid cleaning solutions. If a simple vacuum cleaning is out of the question, try this dry cleaning method to lose the dust and dirt. Pour ½ cup cornmeal and ¼ cup salt into a large paper bag. Place the floral piece into the bag and roll down the top of the bag to form a seal. Shake the bag gently several times. Remove the piece from the bag and carefully brush away any lingering grains of cornmeal or salt.

Spritz Away Burnout Fritz

Whether you spend all day in a home office, classroom, or other location, the air can become stale by mid-day, leaving you feeling sluggish. Closed windows and dry heat in cold climates, or climate controlled environments in office buildings and hotels do little to help circulate air. In fact, the only things that may be circulating in these surroundings are germs! Steel yourself against airborne bacteria and brighten your mood and energy level at the same time with these simple herbal room spritzers.

No-Flame Gel Candles

These candles lend their scent without having to light them, making them perfect to travel with or to use at home without worrying about small children or pets coming into contact with an open flame. If you keep a lid on the gel candle when it's not in use, the scent should last for several weeks.

- 1 **cup cool water, divided**
- 1 **package gelatin mix**
- ⅛ **teaspoon vodka**
- ½ **teaspoon essential oil of choice**

Bring ½ cup of the water to a boil. Add the gelatin to the boiling water, stirring to dissolve. Add the remaining ½ cup of cool water and stir again. Add the vodka and essential oil and stir until well blended. Pour into a clean glass jar and allow the gel candle to set for about 30 minutes. To use, place the gel candle on a shelf, table, or windowsill, but avoid placing it in direct sunlight or near heat. Keep a lid on the candle when not in use to extend its shelf life.

Warm & Cozy Room Spritzer

Perfect for those cold winter days when you could use a little extra warmth. As an added benefit, allspice is antiseptic, antibacterial, antifungal, and antiviral.

1   **cup water**
15   **drops allspice essential oil**
10   **drops cinnamon leaf essential oil**

Combine all ingredients in a small plastic spray bottle. Spritz 2–3 times from the center of the room outward in all directions. Shake well before each use.

TELEPHONE DIRTY TALK TAMER

If you share your home office with other members of the family, you may be sharing germs when you reach for the telephone as well. This formula will stop the bacteria in its tracks. Mix 2 tablespoons water with 2 drops rosemary essential oil and 2 drops tea tree essential oil. Blend all ingredients in a small bowl or cup. Moisten a soft cloth with this solution and clean the telephone receiver. Use a second cloth or towel to dry it off.

Clear the Air Room Spritzer

This combination provides a fresh, clean scent that won't over-power your senses.

1 **cup water**
15 **drops thyme essential oil**
10 **drops sage essential oil**

Combine all ingredients in a small plastic spray bottle. Shake a few times before using and spray in each direction from the center of the room.

ON THE ROAD, CLEAN AND GREEN

* Take along some all-purpose wipes when you're on the road. They're perfect to use in the car, at school, work, or when you're staying at a hotel.
* Use herbal spritzers to sanitize stuffy air in conference rooms or classrooms, or to freshen hotel linens.
* Bring gel candles with you to improve the scent and the ambiance. They travel well, provided they are kept away from direct heat.

RESOURCES

Essential Oils & Dried Herbs

These companies sell essential oils, dried herbs, and herbalist supplies, such as droppers, glassware, labels, bags, and more. In addition to being online, many companies have print catalogs available; call to request one.

APHRODISIA HERB SHOPPE
212-989-6440
www.aphrodisiaherbshoppe.com

AROMA VERA
800-669-9514
www.aromavera.com

AURA CACIA
319-227-7996
www.auracacia.com

AVENA BOTANICALS
866-282-8362
www.avenaherbs.com

BLESSED MAINE HERB FARM
www.blessedmaineherbs.com

BLOSSOM FARM
www.blossomfarm.com

CEDARBROOK LAVENDER AND HERB FARM
800-470-8423
www.cedarbrookherbfarm.com

DESERT ESSENCE
800-848-7331
www.desertessence.com

THE ESSENTIAL OIL COMPANY
800-729-5912
www.essentialoil.com

FROM NATURE WITH LOVE
800-520-2060
www.fromnaturewithlove.com

GOODWIN CREEK GARDENS
800-846-7359
www.goodwincreekgardens.com

THE HERBFARM
425-485 5300
www.theherbfarm.com

LADYBUG HERBS OF VERMONT
802-888-5940
www.ladybugherbsofvermont.com

LIVING EARTH HERBS
360-734-3207
www.livingearthherbs.com

MORNING SUN HERB FARM
707-451-9406
www.morningsunherbfarm.com

MOUNTAIN ROSE HERBS
800-879-3337
www.mountainroseherbs.com

MULBERRY CREEK HERB FARM
419-433-6126
www.mulberrycreek.com

NICHOLS GARDEN NURSERY
800-422-3985
www.nicholsgardennursery.com

SUMMER'S PAST FARMS
619-390-1523
www.summerspastfarms.com

WELL-SWEEP HERB FARM
908-852-5390
www.wellsweep.com

CALDREA
877-576-8808
www.caldrea.com

Nontoxic Cleaning Supplies

These companies distribute safe cleaning products and supplies. In addition to being online, many companies have print catalogs available; call to request one.

DR. BRONNER'S MAGIC SOAPS
760-743-2211
www.drbronner.com

LIFE TREE PRODUCTS
800-824-6396
www.lifetreeproducts.com

METHOD
866-931-3947
www.methodhome.com

MRS. MEYER'S CLEAN DAY
877-865-1508
www.mrsmeyers.com

NATURALLY YOURS
888-801-7347
www.naturallyyoursstore.com

NATURE'S EARTH PRODUCTS
800-749-7463
www.naturesearth.com

NORTH STAR NATURAL PET PRODUCTS
802-446-2812
www.northstarpetsonline.com

PLANET NATURAL
800-289-6656
www.planetnatural.com

SEA SIDE NATURALS
800-870-1697
www.seasidenaturals.com

SEVENTH GENERATION
800-456-1191
www.seventhgeneration.com

SOUND EARTH
888-608-9678
www.soundearth.com

SUN AND EARTH
800-298-7861
www.sunandearth.com

Washing Soda, Grated Soap & Supplies

MSO DISTRIBUTING
888-508-3496
www.msodistributing.com

SOAPS GONE BUY
888-858-7627
www.soapsgonebuy.com

Environmentally Safe Paints

These companies sell paint that is nontoxic or significantly less toxic than commercial brands.

BIO-SHIELD PAINT COMPANY
800-621-2591
www.bioshieldpaint.com

ECO-HOUSE, INC.
877-326-4687
www.eco-house.com

THE OLD FASHIONED MILK-PAINT COMPANY, INC.
866-350-6455
www.milkpaint.com

Safe Pet Products & Supplies

HALO, PURELY FOR PETS
800-426-4256
www.halopets.com

NATURA PET
800-532-7261
www.naturapet.com

NATURE'S EARTH PRODUCTS
www.naturesearth.com

ONLY NATURAL PET
888-937-6677
www.onlynaturalpet.com

PET ALIVE
877-289-1235
www.petalive.com

P.O.R.G.I.E. NATURAL PET SUPPLY
www.porgienaturalhealth.com

Natural Garden & Lawn Products

DIRT WORKS
877-213-3828
www.dirtworks.net

EXTREMELY GREEN GARDENING COMPANY
781-878-5397
www.extremelygreen.com

GARDENS ALIVE
513-354-1482
www.gardensalive.com

HOME HARVEST
517-332-3688
www.homeharvest.com

NAPIER ENVIROMENTAL TECHNOLOGIES
800-663-9274
www.biowash.com

INDEX

Page numbers in **bold** indicate charts.

Other Storey Titles You Will Enjoy

The Aromatherapy Companion, by Victoria H. Edwards.
The most comprehensive aromatherapy guide,
filled with profiles of essential oils and recipes
for beauty, health, and well-being.
288 pages. Paper. ISBN 978-1-58017-150-2.

The One Minute Cleaner Plain & Simple, by Donna Smallin.
The perfect handbook for busy people — clean smarter,
not harder!
288 pages. Paper. ISBN 978-1-58017-659-0.

Organic Body Care Recipes, by Stephanie Tourles.
Homemade, herbal formulas for glowing skin,
hair, and nails, plus a vibrant self.
384 pages. Paper. ISBN 978-1-58017-676-7.

The Organic Lawn Care Manual, by Paul Tukey.
A comprehensive volume of natural lawn-care
information to answer the growing demand for
organic grass.
256 pages. Paper. ISBN 978-1-58017-649-1.
Hardcover. ISBN 978-1-58017-655-2.

Rosemary Gladstar's Herbal Recipes for Vibrant Health,
by Rosemary Gladstar.
A practical compendium of herbal lore and
know-how for wellness, longevity, and bound-
less energy.
408 pages. Paper. ISBN 978-1-60342-078-5.

These and other books from Storey Publishing are available
wherever quality books are sold or by calling 1-800-441-5700.
Visit us at www.storey.com.